Lorilee writes with both lightness and depth, and I found myself completely taken by all three stories—hers, Phoebe's, Anne's. The beauty of her storytelling and the tenderness of the events she describes make this a thoroughly rich reading experience. Well done, Lorilee!

SHAUNA NIEQUIST
Author of *Bread & Wine* and *Savor*

To say it as Anne of Green Gables would, this encouraging book will be a "bosom friend" to your heart!

HOLLEY GERTH
Bestselling author of *You're Already Amazing*

We are *all* enamored by the plight of orphans and gobble up their tales in the wide world of literature. Perhaps we each see ourselves—our fears of abandonment and creases of inadequacy—in their stories. Gently and with honest vulnerability, Lorilee Craker weaves the universal discoveries of orphan Anne into her own very personal story of being an orphan and adopting one. Open the cover. Turn the pages. You'll come out the other end glad for the read and deepened by the journey.

ELISA MORGAN
Speaker; author of *The Beauty of Broken* and *Hello, Beauty Full*

In this artful tapestry, Lorilee Cracker—consummate wordsmith—gifts readers with a beautifully woven journey into the human heart. For her tender vulnerability, creative insight, and beautiful sentences, I highly recommend Cracker's moving memoir.

MARGOT STARBUCK
Author of *The Girl in the Orange Dress*

Lorilee Craker's *"Anne of Green Gables," My Daughter and Me* is a deeply personal memoir about the search for identity that will strike a chord in all of us. Readers will feel as if they're sitting on the couch beside Craker, flipping through family photo albums, as the author shares the touching—and funny!—story of her adoption, that of her daughter's, and the impact of a red-headed "Anne with an e" heroine who lit the path ahead of them in the direction of true belonging.

SUZANNE WOODS FISHER
Bestselling author of *The Heart of the Amish*

With sparkling prose and charming wit, Lorilee Craker takes us on a journey where lives past, present, and fictional intertwine on the path to finding a place of belonging. Grab a cup of raspberry cordial, curl up on the window seat, and join their pilgrimage. You won't be disappointed.

JENNIFER ERIN VALENT
Christy Award–winning author of *Fireflies in December*

An absolute must-read for anyone who loved *Anne of Green Gables* as a girl! Anne's resilience combined with all of her big feelings gave me that trusted bosom-friend as I transitioned from girlhood to womanhood. And now Lorilee offers me the grown-up lens with which to view the scars I bear, the battle wounds of life, as a woman who is not defined by my abandonment but by my adoption into God's family.

ALEXANDRA KUYKENDALL
Author of *The Artist's Daughter*; specialty content editor, MOPS International

"Anne of Green Gables," My Daughter, and Me is a deeply satisfying read, shining brightly with author Lorilee Craker's personality and wit. For those of us who have adopted children, Craker concludes that we cannot rescue or fix them, but—like all parents—we can communicate to our children how worthy they are of God's abundant love.

JENNIFER GRANT
Author of *Love You More, MOMumental, Disquiet Time* (coeditor), and *Wholehearted Living*

With her characteristic spunk, sharp wit, and empathetic lens, Lorilee Craker peels back the layers of the heart in this uniquely woven cross-generational tale. Blending both humor and humility, Craker serves as the voice of the orphan in us. Lovely, lyrical, and laugh-out-loud funny . . . this uplifting memoir is a must-read.

JULIE CANTRELL
New York Times bestselling author of *Into the Free* and *When Mountains Move*

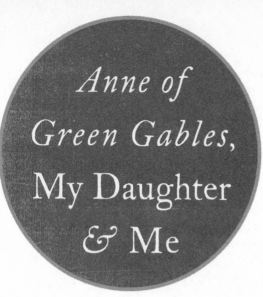

Anne of Green Gables, My Daughter & Me

What My
Favorite Book
Taught Me
about Grace,
Belonging
& the Orphan
in Us All

A Memoir
—

LORILEE CRAKER

TYNDALE®
MOMENTUM

An Imprint of
Tyndale House Publishers, Inc.

Visit Tyndale online at www.tyndale.com.

Visit Tyndale Momentum online at www.tyndalemomentum.com.

Visit the author's website at LorileeCraker.com.

Tyndale Momentum and the Tyndale Momentum logo are registered trademarks of Tyndale House Publishers, Inc., Carol Stream, IL 60188. Tyndale Momentum is an imprint of Tyndale House Publishers, Inc.

Published in association with the literary agency of The Fedd Agency, Inc., P.O. Box 341973, Austin, TX 78734.

Library of Congress Cataloging-in-Publication Data

Craker, Lorilee.

Anne of Green Gables, my daughter, and me : what my favorite book taught me about grace, belonging, and the orphan in us all / Lorilee Craker.

pages cm

Includes bibliographical references.

ISBN 978-1-4964-0343-8 (sc)

1. Craker, Lorilee—Family.   2. Adopted children.   3. Adoptees—Biography.   4. Shirley, Anne (Fictitious character)   5. Montgomery, L. M. (Lucy Maud), 1874-1942. Anne of Green Gables.   6. Families.   I. Title.

HV874.82.C73A3 2015

362.734092—dc23

[B]   2015019549

Printed in the United States of America

21	20	19	18	17	16	15
7	6	5	4	3	2	1

Dedicated to the Matthew Cuthberts in our lives:

Grandpa George Vanderlaan

and the memory of

Marv Besteman.

And to my girl, now and always,

Phoebe Min-Ju Jayne.

Contents

"All 'Spirit and Fire and Dew'": An Introduction *ix*

1 A Couple of "Severe Mental Jolts" *1*

2 "I Love Her Best When She Is Asleep and Better Still When She Is Awake" *11*

3 Vanquishing Josie Pye *21*

4 A Kindred Spirit *37*

5 He Shouldn't Have Called Her "Carrots," But Oh, That Gilbert Blythe! *53*

6 Finding Clara Macneill *67*

7 Bereft, Left Alone, and Left (Two Birth Mothers and Daughters) *81*

8 Dispatches from the Land of Morning Calm *99*

9 "Lawful Heart, Did Anyone Ever See Such Freckles?" *113*

10 I Love My Adopted Child Biologically *127*

11 Reunion Vignettes *133*

12 Raspberry Cordial and Redemption in a Bottle of Ipecac Syrup *151*

13 Finding Walter Shirley *163*

14 Dear Tom *179*

15 (He Did Not Say Dear) Lorilee *187*

16 Twenty Pounds of Brown Sugar and a Garden Rake *195*

17 A Bend in the Road *207*

Acknowledgments *225*

Discussion Guide *229*

Notes *233*

About the Author *239*

I will not leave you as orphans; I will come to you.

JOHN 14:18

*I would not forget you! See, I have written your
name on the palms of my hands.*

ISAIAH 49:15-16, NLT

"All 'Spirit and Fire and Dew'": An Introduction

Anne is an amazing character. She represents something really profound for
people considering she is an orphaned, undervalued, displaced soul, who is told
she is trash. And Anne's certainly the wrong gender to have value in the world.
However, she turns around a community by absolutely remaining true to her spirit.

MEGAN FOLLOWS, LEAD ACTRESS IN THE
ANNE OF GREEN GABLES MINISERIES

"WHAT'S AN ORPHAN?"

The question, posed by my once-parentless kid, left me momentarily speechless. Seven-year-old Phoebe Min-Ju Jayne, she of the raven's wing hair, golden skin, and human cannonball tendencies, asked for the definition as we were reading a children's picture-book version of *Anne of Green Gables* one evening at bedtime.

Since my husband and I retrieved that gorgeous baby—a firecracker even at six months—from Korea, our world had never been the same. P, like Anne, is "all 'spirit and fire and dew,'"[1] a lightning flash who broke off and then nuked the microwave knob (we use pliers to this day) at age two; ran naked through our church at age four; and somehow reversed Grandpa's vintage convertible and rolled it down the driveway, barely averting catastrophe, at age five. Wild thing, she makes our hearts sing—sing, or stop cold five times a day.

Because Phoebe had been abandoned by her birth father while still in the womb and then bravely relinquished by her birth mother in Korea, Phoebe was our girl now. Yet I knew her casual question was one of great magnitude. The word *orphan* is six letters fraught with baggage (and by "baggage," I mean steamer trunk). The evocations are instant and panoramic, bringing up visions of vulnerable ragamuffins who are hungry, desperate, and alone. In our mind's eye, we see a grimy urchin on the streets of Mumbai or a spindly, underdeveloped child, rattling his crib bars in an Eastern European orphanage. Orphans from literature and movies flit across our consciousness. Annie ("Leapin' lizards!"), Harry Potter, Elsa from *Frozen*, Pip from *Great Expectations*, Tarzan, Luke Skywalker—and on and on the orphan archetype goes, all bound up in a great big Oliver Twist–tie. Superman, Batman, Spider-Man, Robin, The Flash, Captain Marvel, Captain America, and Green Arrow: all orphaned!

Yet this word trips wires like almost no other. Adoptive mothers are especially sensitive to it. I once read an emotional blog by a mom in the process of adopting kids from Haiti. She just *loathed* that her I-600 immigration paperwork was stamped with the words "Petition to Classify Orphan as an Immediate Relative."

"The fact that the word *orphan* will describe you for a portion of your life breaks my heart," she wrote. "It seems to signify that you're lost, unclaimed and not cared for." Her heart was yelling like a crazed fan at a hockey game: "I found you! I claim you! I will care for you!" A friend of mine, an adoptive mom, visibly bristled at the word when I brought it up; her eyes grew cold, and her arms folded around herself. Our conversation grounded to a screeching halt. After another friend lost both of her parents in a short span, she prickled when a coworker commented that she was "an orphan now."

Many adoption agencies shy away from or even ban the use of the word in their processes with adopting parents because it's not "positive adoption language." Nobody wants the big fat "orphan" label tattooed to their foreheads or those of their children. Nobody wants to lug around that steamer trunk, for themselves or their kids.

But, if I may reference Inigo Montoya from *The Princess Bride*, I do not think *orphan* means what we think it means.[2] Yes, the common usage is the loss of parents, or at the very least, the abandonment by unfit, living parents. (Interestingly, in the Bible, the word occurs forty-two times, and it always refers to someone without a father; yet in terms of the animal world, orphans are almost always deserted by their mothers.) The word is so much broader and more expansive than we give it credit for. One thesaurus' listing of words related to *orphan*[3] popped out at me in neon:

Orphan: Bereft, left behind, and left.

Bereft.

Left behind.

Left.

By that definition, we've all been orphans at one time or another. We've all been brought to our knees by the loss of someone we love, somebody whose death bereaves us terribly. We've all been left behind, renounced, ditched, and forsaken. Fired. Dumped. Snubbed. And who among us has not been just plain *left*, plopped down on the curb of life, waiting for the ride that will never come?

This definition of orphan shifted my thinking on the word. It downgraded my response from Big Scary Word to something demystified, broader, relatable. I began to see orphans everywhere, spotting the *bereft* in the grieving daughter, the *left behind* in a teenage boy who doesn't make the baseball team, and the *left* in a divorced friend's eyes.

And with the scaling down of it came a new comfort level and the surprising thought that it's actually positive to talk about the O word. Because in a world of Elsas and Annas, Harry Potters and Miss Peregrine's peculiar children, Batmen and Catwomen, it's going to come up, over and over and over. Adoptees especially are going to wonder on some level where they fit into our culture's constant orphan storytelling. No wonder, then, that *orphan* has become an important word for me and my house. Not only was that girl of my heart asking about it; it's a question I've been asking, in one form or another, for most of my life. After all, I was adopted too.

So when Phoebe asked about the definition of orphan, I tried to put the definition in plain terms and tell her in a way that she could understand—that there are many paths to orphanhood. Anne Shirley was orphaned when her loving, schoolteacher parents, Walter and Bertha, both succumbed to typhoid by the time she was three months old. "And Mommy was an orphan before Oma and Opa adopted her," I explained. "My birth mother couldn't take care of a baby then, just like your birth mom couldn't take care of a baby, any baby, when you came. You were a kind of orphan, too, like me and like Anne, before we came to Korea and brought you home."

"Like Anne . . ." Huh.

That conversation with my daughter lit something in me. We were, all three of us—me, Phoebe Min-Ju Jayne, and Anne—card-carrying castaways who had traveled a winding path to belonging. I've always wanted to tell the quirky, poignant, and oddly paralleled stories of my daughter's and my adoptions. In that moment, cuddled up together on P's bed, I knew I wanted to tell those stories plus one more in a book, braiding each chapter with a devilishly red-haired ribbon.

"Anne of Green Gables," My Daughter, and Me is the result. As I wrote, I wove in one smaller strand, the story of Anne's creator, Lucy Maud Montgomery, who invested her life's work in writing stories about children who felt as lost and alone as she did. "Maud," the child of a mother who died when she was a baby and a mostly absentee father, seemed to be on a quest to find belonging for herself and her characters. As I've read thousands upon thousands of her words,

Maud has become a writing godmother to me. I deeply admire her fat, buttery words, her pitch-perfect references to the Bible and classic literature, and her ability to make me laugh *and* cry. She was a gifted humor writer who had the rare gift of handling both comedy and drama well. Yet she experienced the pummeling rejection known to every writer; *Anne of Green Gables* was rejected several times before being published.[4]

Part memoir and part Anne super-fan book, this book will interlace Anne's and Maud's stories with our yarns, taking you from the red-dirt beaches of Prince Edward Island to the ginseng fields of Korea. Along the way, you may uncover truths about your own search for identity, finding yourself in places you hadn't thought to look.

As you enter Anne's world through quotations from and retellings of a few of her stories, you'll fall under her spell, energized by her heart's vigor and an unsinkable spirit that couldn't be submerged even after she had been sorely bereaved, left alone, and just plain *left*. So full of hope and good humor, she reminds us we can all live our lives as she did—resilient, redemptive, and openhearted. She inspires "orphans" of every kind to find a home that feels right and that may or may not be with our biological relatives.

Since the 1908 release of Maud's first novel, Anne Girl endures—beloved, cherished, and admired, not because Anne is perfect, but rather because she's far from it. We see ourselves in the girl who hopefully uttered the words "tomorrow is a new day with no mistakes in it yet,"[5] wishing for a new day and a clean slate to begin again, or maybe just to break over Gilbert Blythe's cute head. She represents the unwanted stray that exists in all of us from time to time. She makes us believe in ourselves, though we've all been "left" in some essential way. She compels us to keep moving forward, even when it's hard.

Meeting Anne

Most kids lucky enough to grow up with books discover a character who inspires them. Being from the prairies, I thrilled to Laura Ingalls Wilder and her homesteading adventures. And I cheered for that ambitious Little Woman, Josephine March, a prefeminist who wrote her way out of any hole. But I had only one real kindred spirit, a lifelong literary companion. No one could light a candle to the carrotheaded magpie who found her way home to the reluctant care of a lonely, aging brother and sister who discovered they needed her far more than she needed them.

I met Anne around the time I was myself in "the depths of despair,"[6] having fallen victim to an eighth-grade she-bully who blacklisted me for most of the year. I didn't know it would all blow over, as these things usually do, and that by year's end I would find my own Diana Barry, a bosom friend who understood me just as I was. All I knew was that I was so lonely and that school was nearly unbearable. Anne's melodramatic speeches ("My life is a perfect graveyard of buried hopes"[7]) gave voice to my pain; her deep sensitivity to rejection and insult reflected my own. I clung to my literary friend, distracted by her hilarious capers and inspired to find hope and beauty in the cruel ugliness of eighth grade. After all, Anne was able to put that insufferable Josie Pye in her place; maybe I could do the same with Viola Goossen.

Anne was my one true friend during those days and in the days to come. She was me, except that she dreamed of nut-brown hair, and my hair was the exact color of some nut, somewhere, before I started smearing it in various shades of "mochachino." She dreamed of puffed sleeves, and I dreamed of buffed arms. She bemoaned her hair; I bemoaned my thighs. Minor details. Really, I'm a lot like Anne:

- Featherbrained? Check. Especially in the morning. I have to *drink* coffee to *make* coffee.

- Motormouthed? Obviously a check.

- Crazy for Gilbert Blythe? Check, *italicized*, **bolded**, and <u>underlined</u>. My dear husband, Doyle, sometimes jokes that should Gilbert Blythe appear at our door, drawn out of the pages of *Anne of Green Gables*, it will be all over between us.

Three cheers for Anne with an "e"! She is a girl who, give or take hair the color of orange soda and exceptional academic strengths, is my fictional twin. A girl who understands, more than dear Laura Ingalls and Jo March, what it is to be an orphan like me and, later, like my own fiery little girl. Even at my somewhat mature age, I still channel that plucky, dreamy girl who has endless "scope for the imagination."[8] Anne's impassioned spirit emboldens mine, and her sensitivity and boundless imagination mirror my own softhearted dreaminess.

I'm betting you feel the same way about Anne with an "e," that she's *your* kindred spirit too. She means so much to so many people. Come along for the ride as my girl and I step into the world of our favorite book—of reveling in ipecac-soaked drama, sampling liniment-flavored cake, and getting your best friend inadvertently spiffed on raspberry cordial.

Join Anne, me, and Phoebe Min-Ju Jayne as our stories plait together—one strand red, one raven black, and one mochachino. Link arms with us as we find our way to places of belonging, our forever homes. Settle in with us in this world of "spirit and fire and dew." Here's a story for the orphan in us all.

A Couple of "Severe Mental Jolts"

We learned that orphans are easier to ignore before you know their names.
They are easier to ignore before you see their faces. It is easier to pretend they're
not real before you hold them in your arms. But once you do, everything changes.

DAVID PLATT, RADICAL

ON A SMALL CANADIAN PENINSULA protruding into the Atlantic Ocean, the little village of Avonlea was experiencing something of a ripple in the usual flow of things. Matthew Cuthbert, a man who literally never raised eyebrows, including his own, was supposed to be sowing his late turnip seeds at this hour of this day, like every other God-fearing farmer on Prince Edward Island. And yet there he was, at midafternoon, driving out of the village of Avonlea.

What is more, he was wearing his best suit and driving the buggy led by his chestnut-colored horse, as opposed to taking a less formal method of transportation. From this set of clues laid out for readers on the opening pages of *Anne of Green Gables*, Mrs. Rachel Lynde "betokened"[1] that he must be going a long way. This was no common errand her bachelor neighbor was on, and she would not rest easy until she knew where he was headed.

Mrs. Rachel marched out of Lynde's Hollow and walked the quarter mile to Green Gables, the spacious house where the Cuthberts lived, to obtain answers to her burning questions. The home was set so far back on the property that it was scarcely detectable from the main road. Not only was Green Gables hidden, both the house and the yard were painfully clean. "One could have eaten a meal off the ground," we are told, "without overbrimming the proverbial peck of dirt."[2]

Mrs. Rachel Lynde did not approve of such an austere, reclusive house. In fact, in her opinion, inhabiting such a house wasn't *living* in it so much as *staying* in it.[3]

Little did she know that soon enough the staying would melt into living, and this hermetically sealed dwelling situation of which she disapproved was about to bust wide open. No one in Avonlea, including her, would ever be the same.

...

Though not fixed in as picturesque a setting as Green Gables, the bungalow I was brought home to as an infant was nearly as immaculate. It was in that house, located on a humble street of Cold War–era bungalows on Winnipeg's northwest side, that a beauty supply salesman named Abe phoned his wife from work, broaching the subject of adoption. A man he worked with at Monarch Beauty Supply had recently adopted a baby with his wife. He wondered out loud if this might be a solution to their childlessness, now approaching three and a half years since their September wedding day. His wife, a nurse named Linda, said little before replacing the black phone on the wall. The notion was startling, but not unfamiliar. As a labor and delivery nurse, she had cared for many newborns who had been surrendered by their birth mothers. Might one of those babies come to belong to her and Abe? New hope bubbled like a current under her skin.

Linda set a dish of crab apple preserves on the table for supper, picked from their tree in the yard and canned by her own hands. *Adoption.* She tasted the word in her mouth. It wasn't unheard of in broader society; in fact, she knew all those babies at the hospital were adopted by childless couples. But in their culture, their world, it hadn't been done yet. Linda couldn't think of a single relative (and she and Abe had hordes of them) or anyone in their church community who had adopted a child. The baby would not be a Mennonite, ethnically, for Mennonites were more than a denomination; they were a peculiar people, set apart by history, culture, language, and shared beliefs. But did that really matter? Some folks might think so. Some folks might think this was risky business for sure, raising someone who was not your natural child. Who knew what kind of person this baby might grow up to be?

But somehow, Linda didn't care. She knew Abe didn't either. She remembered the excitement in his voice on the phone. They were ready to open their hearts.

Their house, 542 Kingston Avenue, was tidy and small. Much like Marilla Cuthbert's yard, on Linda's watch, "one," too, "could have eaten a meal off the ground without overbrimming the proverbial peck of dirt." Its amenities included a patio; a huge, gnarled poplar tree along with several crab apple trees in the backyard; and a weeping willow tree in the front. Though only four years old, the house had its quirks already—the chief being a bomb shelter in the basement. The previous owners may have built it to protect themselves from Castro or Khrushchev, but the Mennonite salesman's wife used it to house mason jars of crab apples, tomatoes, and cold bean salad. In the future, her children, procured in an unusual way, would become very familiar with the cold, damp space. "Could you please go down to the Bomb Shelter and bring me up two jars of beets?" she would call down the stairs, where they were flopped on the shag rug, watching *Gilligan's Island*. She never failed to refer to it by its given name, and in capital letters. *Bomb Shelter.*

In present day, the kitchen smelled of bay leaves and cabbage, of rhubarb and plums and canning spices, their shared tradition and heritage, 443 years of Mennonite foods and folkways expressed in a kettle of borscht and fruit *platz* with streusel topping.

There were just two empty little bedrooms across the tiny hallway, but castles of space were available in their hearts. Why God had not answered their prayers for children yet was a mystery, a painful reality, yet they believed that He knew best, that His unknowable ways were right and good. Doctors had no answers for them, so they kept praying, together with hands clasped at the supper table, and all alone when nobody knew what they were thinking. When Abe got home from work, they would have a new conversation, the kind in which the old passes away and new life comes.

· · ·

Mrs. Rachel Lynde was silent for a full five seconds when she heard the reason for Matthew Cuthbert's extraordinary errand.

A little boy.

From Nova Scotia.

An *orphan*.

It was almost impossible to find the words to form the whys and wherefores, but Mrs. Rachel was noted for always speaking her mind and finding the words to do so. Usually, she tacked on the words "that's what" to her declarative sentences to add a note of inarguable finality.

We are told that Matthew's going "to meet a kangaroo from Australia"[4] might have been a less flabbergasting development. We are also told that there was a dish of crab apple preserves on the table, already set for Matthew's return with the orphan boy from Nova Scotia.

As Marilla, Matthew's sister, ticked off her reasons for adopting an orphan from the asylum, Mrs. Rachel could only stare in horror. Mrs. Alexander Spencer, a respectable woman known to them both, was going to adopt a little girl at the same time. She was charged with selecting a boy for them and bringing this boy to them on her way back home.

At age sixty, Matthew was troubled by his heart and therefore challenged to do the farm work that a hired hand might help with, if hired hands were easy to find, which they were not.

Matthew and Marilla had come to the conclusion that adopting a boy to help on the farm would pose a solution to their problems. If they got a boy around ten or eleven, he would be the perfect age to accomplish chores right off, and young enough to be raised up proper. They meant to give him a respectable home and schooling. The brother and sister had received a telegram from Mrs. Spencer that morning. The orphan boy was on the 5:30 train that very after-noon, and Matthew was on his way to pick him up.

Mrs. Rachel was rendered all but catatonic by this news. She received, we are told, a "severe mental jolt,"[5] and felt that nothing would shock her after this. *Nothing!*

In Avonlea, one good verbal thumping deserved another, and Mrs. Rachel pelted Marilla with disapproval, all but bopping her about the head with reasons why she had clearly gone insane. Marilla Cuthbert, she of hard angles and graying hair brought up in a stiff knot with two hairpins jammed through it, of restricted experience and straitlaced morals, of the saving grace of a mouth that suggested a sense of humor, took the onslaught like a chief.

She was expecting Mrs. Rachel's disapproval and had thought through some of the same talking points her neighbor brought up. This is because the talking points Mrs. Rachel brought up are the same viewpoints, worries, and opinions that have been brought up about orphans since time immemorial. According to Mrs. Rachel and home pundits over the centuries, adopting an orphan is foolish, reckless, risky, and unsafe because of the following:

You're allowing a stranger into your house and home.

This stranger has an unknowable temperament and hails from a mysterious ancestry. (Why, he could be from a family of lunatics! Hairy people! Circus people! Grits! Tories! Democrats! Republicans!)

Mrs. Rachel, like so many others, allowed her imagination to mosey down a long dark alley of possibilities, where she was jumped every few steps. How many potential mothers and fathers and families allow themselves to be taken hostage by the unknown (and mostly untrue)?

She continued with the nugget of the thing: You don't know how this little stranger—this potentially deranged fire-eater who supports the wrong political party because it is in his very *blood*—will turn out, *that's what*. You don't know what the outcome will be, *that's what*. (Obviously, people over the centuries have been able to predict with 100 percent accuracy how their genetic posterities will turn out.)

And that is the deal breaker for most people, including Mrs. Rachel.

Not that she took a breath, but I believe Mrs. Rachel might have noted that Marilla seemed unmoved by her theories and *that's whats*. So she pulled out the big guns, the horror stories, the tales of orphans past that should have caused those two hairpins to pop right out of Marilla's tightly wound head.

Just the week before, Mrs. Rachel said that she read in the paper how a couple had taken in a boy out of an orphanage. The boy set fire to the house at night—*deliberately*! That innocent couple was nearly fried alive in their own beds.

She knew of another case (of course she did) where an adopted boy sucked the whites and yolks out of eggs, just slurped the ever-loving dilly out of them and could not be broken of the vile habit. (On the bright side, he did not have a protein deficiency.)

"If you had asked my advice in the matter—which you didn't do, Marilla—I'd have said for mercy's sake not to think of such a thing, that's what."[6]

Marilla, with hairpins still intact, remained unmoved. Mrs. Rachel saved the *pièce de résistance* for last, a story she must unleash for Marilla's own good.

"Well, I hope it will turn out all right,"[7] Mrs. Rachel said in a way that suggested there was no way it would. She then begged Marilla, "Don't say I didn't warn you,"[8] should she find herself burnt to a crisp in her bed or possessed of hundreds of vacant eggs, unusable for custard pie.

But there was a worse fate than these, and Mrs. Rachel laid this one on her friend with all the righteous indignation in her being:

The Case of Strychnine in the Well.

Strychnine, you ask? A darling of literature (Sir Arthur Conan Doyle and Agatha Christie both made great use of it in their literary murders), strychnine is essentially rat poison that is often fatal when ingested. Mrs. Rachel told Marilla she had heard about an orphan asylum child in New Brunswick who had poisoned a well, leading an entire family to die in appalling anguish. (One can assume that Mrs. Rachel's tone left no doubt that she feared the siblings Cuthbert would shuffle off this mortal coil in similar, appalling fashion.)

"Only it was a girl in that instance,"[9] she added, just to be fair.

A girl. Marilla and Matthew had distinctly asked for a boy, not a girl. So, really, there was nothing to be concerned about, was there?

...

I know something of Matthew's astonishment when the stationmaster informed him that the orphan he'd come to pick up was in fact the earnest little girl sitting on a stack of shingles and not the boy he had expected. My surprise came in a sterile hospital delivery room on the southeast side of Grand Rapids, Michigan, on the day my second baby boy was born. That was the same day that I imagined a baby girl with gemstone clarity for the first time.

The ultrasound technician had told me this infant was a girl, in utero. And so the baby's closet was crammed with pink footie sleepers and other girlie loot, every befrilled outfit given as gifts from others. Doyle and I had chosen the name Phoebe for our expected daughter, a name we both thought was the bee's knees. To us, it was golden, not too popular, and not too weird. We wanted to unearth a vintage treasure, a biblical name that meant "bright shining star." I was still somewhat hung up on Ruby, my other favorite at the time, and waffling a bit, but Doyle insisted.

"Phoebe is the name of a bird, too," he said. Doyle digs birds. That somehow sealed the deal. Plus, the ancient Phoebe mentioned in Romans 16 was a leader in the early church and the apostle Paul's emissary to the Romans. I dig that, a lot. A Titan in Greek mythology, a bird, a bright shining star! We would bestow all of this on our daughter's tiny shoulders, a mantle of history, story, and meaning.

Yet here was our second son, screaming blue murder, enraged yet exquisite. His older brother, three-year-old Jonah, was in the safekeeping of his doting Grandma Pat and Grandpa George at that moment.

I must have known somehow that the ultrasound technician was off when she had said she thought most likely we were having a girl. "I can't get a perfect shot, but as you can see—" she pointed to a nebulous blotch on the screen—"I'm pretty sure we are having a girl here."

Doyle and I nodded as if that amorphous blob told an indisputable story. We bobbed our heads in agreement to seeing something we did not see. She was the one wielding the squeeze bottle of ultrasound gel, after all.

Obviously, she was misinformed.

I wanted a girl, a daughter, with every cell of my being but had not allowed myself to totally surrender to the possibilities. On some level, I knew. Even as I wrote thank-you notes to people, and laundered and folded flowery wee ensembles, I was aware that something was skew-whiff with the girl theory.

Dr. Grey's announcement "It's a boy," then, was not the severe mental jolt it might have been. Oh, we were definitely jostled, just not *completely* rattled to our foundations. Doyle and I both shot each other wide-eyed looks.

"*Whaaaaaat? A boy?*" It still gave us a good few minutes of quaking.

My first thought was that now I could use the boy name I loved. I'm not a name freak for nothing. I had a grand boy's name tucked away just in case my instinct was right and this baby did not turn out to be a Phoebe. *Ezra.* Ezra Finney Brandt Craker. Ezra, because it was poetic and robust and still original in our neck of the woods; it was also old-fashioned, rare, and biblical, like our firstborn's name, Jonah. The name possessed a certain offbeat quality and zest for life we liked and hoped to impart to our new son. Finney was after Doyle's beloved Grandma and Grandpa Finney, and Brandt was my cherished grandma's maiden name. A one-of-a-kind name for a one-of-a-kind boy. I adored him to the moon from that first quaking moment.

In that delivery room at Metropolitan Hospital on Grand Rapids' southeast side, we were expecting a girl and received a boy instead. It was the exact opposite of Matthew and Marilla's situation.

The difference is, in my case, I also received a daughter. My next thought, after the boy surprise; the name delight; and the love for him that broke over me like a surf, was a revelation. We were going to adopt a girl someday.

An old African proverb says that children have two birthdays: the day they are born, and the day when they are first envisioned by their mothers. December 19, 2000, the day we welcomed our baby boy into the world, was also a birthing day for Phoebe. I settled in with Ezra, holding his warmth and sweetness next to my skin and put thoughts of another child aside for the time being. I didn't know who, and I didn't know when or where, but a radiant knowledge had taken root: A bright shining star was coming to us all.

"I Love Her Best When She Is Asleep and Better Still When She Is Awake"

Perhaps there are those who are able to go about their lives unfettered by such concerns. But for those like us, our fate is to face the world as orphans, chasing through long years the shadows of vanished parents.

KAZUO ISHIGURO, *WHEN WE WERE ORPHANS*

BERTHA SHIRLEY'S EYES WERE SO EXPRESSIVE "she could just about talk with" them.[1] She was twenty years old and married to her love, the awkward yet sincere Walter. They had one little baby, bright-eyed Anne, who had appropriated both their hearts upon her birth. Anne had belonged to Walter and Bertha for three blissful months.

Bertha, who had been a much-loved teacher for several years before giving birth to Anne, possessed the ability to write letters as expressive as her eyes. Her personality shone through her words, preserving their splendor and bouquet years after they were written. Bertha had left fewer than a dozen letters, each one an epistle of love to Walter, a collection of words and story consecrated by their incalculable meaning to her daughter. By the time Anne first laid eyes on these notes, she was grown. Still, the letters were a treasure to her, even though they held the patina of decades—yellowed and blurry, discolored and crinkly, but still readable.

The dearest letter of all was the last one, which Bertha wrote to Walter very soon after their baby was born, when Walter had to be away for some reason. Bertha's pride in "'baby'—her cleverness, her brightness, her thousand sweetnesses"[2] knew no bounds. This new mother had no idea that someday her baby would read her words of devotion and be affected to her very marrow.

Bertha ended her letter with this postscript: "I love her best when she is asleep and better still when she is awake."[3] It may have been the last sentence she had ever written. Bertha soon contracted typhoid (or maybe she had it already when the letter was written?), and she was at the departure gate, waiting for the angels.[4]

We know that Walter died soon after Bertha, leaving baby Anne on her own, bereft, left behind, and left, in a way we can hardly grasp in this day and age. When I first reread *Anne of the Island* as a mother, it just about killed me. How awful to leave this earth without a good plan for your baby! It also made me think that so many things would have been different today. If a young couple, both twenty years of age, died leaving a baby, there would be lots of possible solutions, but back then there were few. Even so, it is tragic to consider that there was *no one* on either side of Anne's family to take her in. Even in the age of typhoid, cholera, and consumption, it seems unlikely that there wasn't even a grumpy set of grandparents to take her in, as in Maud's case, after her mother died. Wasn't there even a crotchety great-aunt? A second cousin, once removed?

(By the way, nobody writes cantankerous biddies like our Maud. Rachel Lynde is just the tip of the iceberg. From Mrs. Rachel to Marilla Cuthbert, Aunt Mary Maria Blythe, Susan Baker, and Miss Cornelia—these hilarious and crusty old crabs are the salt of Avonlea's earth—not to mention Glen St. Mary and Maud's other burgs.)

Yet Anne was left behind, wholly orphaned. I'm pretty sure this was a plot device on Maud's part, because had Walter and Bertha survived typhoid there would have been no Matthew, Marilla, Gilbert, or Diana. Anne's orphanhood was the path that brought her to Prince Edward Island, to eight books, and to fifty million copies sold.

There was no one to take baby Anne and give her a decent, loving upbringing. There was no Child and Family Services to scoop her up, monitor her care, and find her a family in which to belong. There was no one to arrange emergency foster care for her as a stopgap measure. Adoption did not exist in the way we think of it today, as a formal intention to transfer all the rights of parenthood to people whose goal is to love the child as their own. In fact, The Foundling Asylum in New York City, begun by three nuns to provide care for abandoned infants, opened in 1869, four years after Anne's birth. The home's first recorded adoption occurred in 1873, the first step to realizing their goal of placing all their children in permanent and loving settings. In the nineteenth century, *adoption* was really another word for indenture, service, and labor—it was glorified slavery puffed up in a thin disguise of good works.

Baby Anne was deeply vulnerable, her position weaker than a kitten's. In her day, concern for animal welfare came earlier than concern for children's welfare. According to an appendix in *The Annotated Anne of Green Gables*, the Society for the Prevention of Cruelty to Animals was founded in 1824 in Nova Scotia, but the care of abused and neglected children wasn't addressed until 1880, when a provincial act passed.[5]

Anne as a stray waif didn't even have the rights of a stray dog. The lines between orphanages, poorhouses, and mental asylums were so blurred, she could have easily ended up in a place like the Halifax poorhouse of 1900, where orphan children lived in quarters without locks or handles on the doors, among criminals and the mentally unstable. Had she been taken to an orphanage as an infant, she still would have been at risk, as mortality rates in such places were appalling. In 1875, for example, the year after Maud was born, the infant mortality rate at the Halifax Infant Home was 35 percent.[6]

What did happen was that the woman who worked as a char-lady for Walter and Bertha Shirley stepped in and took baby Anne, answering to no one about it because no one cared. Even when our family adopted the mutt we affectionately call Junie the Wonder Dog, we had to be approved by the Humane Society as fit owners; yet no one approved or disapproved Mrs. Thomas as Anne's foster mother. Today, a good social worker would never allow Mrs. Thomas and her drunk, abusive husband to take home a hamster, never mind a baby girl. When things fell apart for the Thomases, Anne's owner-ship (because let's call it what it was) was transferred to the equally unworthy Hammonds, a shambles of a household and family, with more work and less care for Anne.

And finally, for the last four months of her life before Green Gables, eleven-year-old Anne was transferred to the asylum in Hopeton, an orphanage patterned after the asylum in Halifax. Reformers of the day hoped for an asylum to live up to its name as a refuge, haven, and sanctuary, but the orphans still weren't loved. At last Anne had reliable food and shelter and schooling, but she still had a ways to go before she was to find her place of belonging.

...

I called my mum recently to wish her a happy fiftieth anniversary (a hard day for her, since my dad passed away in 2006). We ended up talking about my adoption and our beginnings as a family.

"You only cost eight dollars," she said. "I just saw the receipt the other day. Can you believe it? And you only took twelve days."

Before I could digest the fact that I came with a receipt, Mum went on.

"Did I ever tell you what happened when we went to pick you up?" (No.)

"It was the strangest thing. We got to the hospital and there was no one around; not a single staff person was there. We waited and waited. Finally, we just took you home. Mind you, we *did* call to say we had taken you. They seemed glad that we called, but they told us it was fine, that they were happy we had taken you."

My mum is the world's ultimate rule follower. She's a teetotaler, a woman who is troubled lest a blouse neckline be construed as "brief" when it dips a millimeter below her clavicle. She does not jaywalk, feed the animals at the zoo, or snip the warning tag off new pillows. This same woman was now telling me she and my dad, the world's number-two ultimate rule follower, had swiped a newborn from a hospital and brought her home without express permission from the authorities. Had she said I had been raised by polar bears in the Arctic for the first few years of my life, I might have been less surprised.

In 1968, when I was adopted, my parents had their pick of babies. Literally, they were told to come on down to the Women's Pavilion and pick out the newborn they wanted to take home. It was like a baby farm in those days. Rows of babies were swaddled in blankets like husks of corn, the daughters and sons of unwed mothers, eight dollars per bundle. A bumper crop of babies was available for pickup, though they did not deliver. But this pick-out-your-own-baby business rubbed my dad the wrong way.

"We're not buying a cow here!" he told the social worker on the phone. "You pick out our baby, and that will be God's choice for us." Apparently the social worker made his selection, which was approved by God Himself, but no official staff person was there to validate the transaction. I was two weeks old.

It was the Invasion of the Mennonite Baby Snatchers, a piece of my history I had previously not known about. Of course, Abe and Linda being Abe and Linda, and Mennonites being Mennonites, they made terrible baby snatchers and called the hospital as soon as they got home, took off their shoes, and placed them side by side on the rubber mat by the door. "I was kind of worried the police might be following us!" my mum said brightly, as if this infant pinching episode had been kind of a madcap caper.

She can't remember exactly what was happening at the hospital, if I was in a bassinet in the lobby, waiting for pickup, or if I was one of a number of infants in some kind of nursery, left unattended for a period long enough for my rule-following parents to give up and grab me. "But we must have known that you were the baby we were supposed to take home," she said solemnly, as if I might worry that perhaps they nicked the wrong one. "Maybe our name was on your crib!"

She and I both paused to reflect on this extraordinary meeting of parents and child.

"Boy," she said, her tone contemplative, "nowadays that would have caused quite a ruckus."

For this pair of lambs, the radical action they took that day in 1968 was ruckus enough. I picture my dad wearing a suit with his light-brown hair slicked back and my mum wearing a dress and sporting a black beehive, both excited and scared as their dream of parenthood is about to be made manifest in a baby so small, so prune-like. I remember my dad saying he was terrified I wouldn't live. Like every new dad, he was afraid he would break me.

In the car, on the way home, I see Mum breaking her gaze only long enough to sneak a peek over her shoulder in case the police should be in hot pursuit just as Dad turns right onto Henderson Highway and onto Kingston Avenue. He drives carefully over the last slushy stretch of street until that twinkling of time when they pull into 542 as a family of three.

My dad hops out of the car and opens the passenger side door for my mum, who carefully wiggles out of the seat, carrying her baby up two steps and over the threshold of her new home.

Someday there would be a wooden playhouse to host a pet mouse, secret societies, and tea parties. There would be a son, Dan, added to the family just a few years later—this time after a fifteen-day wait. There would be a tire swing hanging from the huge old oak tree, and the initials LR and DR etched in wet cement. But now, there was just a simple house with three bedrooms and a bomb shelter, a place to come home to.

Mrs. Lovrossi, an Italian lady on the street that built me, full of immigrants from Germany, Ukraine, and Poland, told me once that my mother changed my outfit four times a day. "You would wear these preety leetle dresses, sometimes with leetle gloves even, and if you got a specka of dirt on your dressa, your mama would peek you up and carry you inside to change your dressa." This is how I know that the second thing my mum did—after listening in on the phone call between my dad and the hospital, and making sure they didn't have to bring me back—was to change my diaper and dress me in the softest, most beautiful baby pajamas their limited money could buy.

She and my dad watched me as I slept, their hearts blowing up in the quiet with love and pride. That night, they loved me best when I was asleep, but they would love me better still each morning I woke up as their daughter.

...

No photo is more scrutinized than that of a child's photo on his or her adoption referral paperwork. No photo, ever. Trust me on this. An adoption referral portrait invites more scrutiny than an online dating photo, more inspection than a sketchy passport at the Ukrainian/ Moldovan border, more analysis than a fake ID at a nightclub. This photo gets stared at one hundred times a day, each feature of the little person analyzed and reanalyzed. No photo is ever more valued and dear.

I was home alone when Phoebe's referral came in an e-mail. It was the end of February 2005, while Doyle was at work and the boys were at school. My heart thumped wildly as I looked at my daughter for the first time. She had black hair, of course; a tiny, perfect nose; and puffy, newborn eyes. I cried as I fell in love, again. Now we had a face to put to our hopes. Her name was Eun Jung, and her birthday was December 30, 2004. *This must be a joke,* I thought. *A third December birthday!* She shared a birthday with her twin cousins, Jadon and Eli, who had turned two the day she was born.

(Dear God, re: three December birthdays, in the same month as Christmas: Ha ha ha! Not funny! Not laughing!)

I called Doyle at work and jumped in the van. I raced to Oakdale School and pulled Ezra out of preschool and Jonah out of first grade. Mrs. Knott, Jonah's seasoned and lovely teacher, hugged me as she agreed this was big stuff; this was worth pulling a seven-year-old boy from his studies; this was the day our family would shape-shift in a significant way. At home, we scrutinized our new member together. I had printed Phoebe's photo and we passed it back and forth. Four-year-old Ezra, who frequently said he missed Phoebe, the baby sister he had never met, was the most taken with the photo. She wasn't just a theory or a phantom anymore; she was a face, a name, a birthday in December. She was ours. We had something to show for our two years of waiting and hoping and filling out more paperwork than it would take to buy three houses.

That night I stared at the picture one more time before placing it beside my bed and turning out the lights. I lay awake for a long time, daydreaming about my two-month-old baby, pining for her. Korea was thirteen hours ahead, so it was broad daylight there, lunchtime. *Is her foster mom giving her a bottle even now?* I was jealous and grateful. I loved Phoebe (Eun Jung!) best when she was a dream and a wish, and even better still when she was a realization.

· 3 ·

Vanquishing Josie Pye

There is a crack in everything.
That's how the light gets in.
LEONARD COHEN, "ANTHEM"

I WAS ABOUT THIRTEEN when I delved into *Anne of Green Gables* for the first time. I had tried reading it a couple of years earlier, but Maud's sophisticated language and thousand-dollar words were too rich for me then. People regard Anne as a children's book, but really, it's well suited to teenagers and adults. It wasn't until years later after a couple of rereadings that I grasped the orphan connection, but I did feel an instant affinity as a young teen to dramatic, dreamy Anne. I adored Matthew's gentle, fatherly ways and rued the fact that I had not been born during the Victorian era and that Gilbert Blythe did not attend my school, the Mennonite Brethren Collegiate Institute. I also felt a strong kinship to Anne's loyal best friend, Diana Barry.

I, too, had experienced the mercy and shelter of a bosom friend. Lori, my best friend from kindergarten through sixth grade, and I were inseparable during those years. Together, we'd fly backward off the monkey bars, practice our loopy *L*s in cursive while sitting in her family's pop-up trailer, and watch *Another World* in her cool basement

21

with her mom and aunts. My family called me Lori, too, so we had the same name. The two Loris belonged to each other in the extraspecial way that all first best friends do.

In seventh grade, Lori and I were set on different paths, she to the local public junior high school and I to the private Mennonite school through which my dad had paid his own way in the 1950s. I was distraught to leave Lori and my other friends, and I begged my parents to let me go on with them, but my parents held firm. They would scrape and save and do without so Dan and I could have braces on our teeth and a private Mennonite education. Eventually, Lori and I drifted apart as kids do when they go to different schools, though we were to become extremely close again as young adults.

By the time I picked up Anne's story in a serious way, I was ready to sit at her feet and learn from a master. She could tutor me in choosing joy, grace, and dreams amid the hopeless, lonely mess my second year at MBCI was becoming. She could show me how to cope with a mean girl whose purpose in life was to make another girl's life miserable. In grade eight, a former friend, Viola Goossen, had turned into my own personal Josie Pye. Snub by snub, jab by jab, I was shrinking into the smallness of a middle-school target girl.

The lowest moment of all came in Mr. Warkentine's math class, my own personal dungeon. When Viola Goossen dropped her pencil case, scattering pens, pencils, and gum wrappers all over the floor near my desk, it seemed to be a chance for me to gain a shred of approval from her. Despite her protests that she could do it, I dropped to the floor and quickly scooped up all the flotsam from her case and stuffed it back in. When I looked in her dark eyes, I saw confusion and disdain, and at once I knew my social standing, which I was trying desperately to boost, had plunged even further. She sat back down at her desk, scribbled and passed a bunch of notes to her cronies, and together they whispered and whispered and whispered.

I was in the middle of an exile that lasted about six months. I didn't know that it would ever end.

It's true I hated Viola with the kind of bone-deep animosity that can only be bred when one junior-high girl turns on another, and then, by the power vested in her by her peers, compels the entire grade eight community to do likewise.

Far beneath the hatred was a layer where old affinity, a tiny pebble of love, lived. A pea under twenty mattresses and twenty feather beds. This made everything worse. If only I could loathe her efficiently, like clean-burning coal, without the sediments of former loyalties and attachments. But there I was, in my dungeon and other places at school, dodging emotional bayonets and wondering how things had gone so wrong between us.

Viola and I used to hold hands at the Sunday school picnic and warble "It Only Takes a Spark" side by side at Pioneer Girls. We whispered confidences after church in the lobby and at the mother/daughter banquet. Viola and I were bonded, not just because we shared a sense of humor and the inability to earn our Pioneer Girls sewing badge. We were both slap-nuts boy crazy, so that probably helped propel our friendship in childhood and repel it in junior high. What we understood about each other went deeper than crushes on the boys at our church: Viola was adopted too. On some level, we understood that we were both "other," that we both had vaporous, exotic birth mothers out there, mothers who were not our mums. We spun a million daydreams on the same spinning wheel.

It's a little bit tragic that Viola and I failed to make the transition from church friends to school friends. Little girls who adored each other, we could have provided such empathy and support for each other in those knotty, messy years of forging an identity. Instead, our posture upon entering the same junior high school was almost instantly that of competitors, first for boys and then for social standing.

She won—no contest. Viola was prettier than I, and she was definitely more confident. Her power was her defining quality in those years. (Where does that come from, that innate supremacy that tolerates no opposition? Why is it obeyed so unswervingly? This mean-girl thing melts my head.)

When Phoebe comes home from school with tales of so-and-so Bee-All, it makes me go all crazy Mama Bear.

"Why does Ava get to tell you that you can't play with Brynn? Who made her the boss?"

"Why do you let Emily form a club with your friends? Who made her the boss?"

Nobody ever seems to have an answer for that question. It makes me want to stomp around and growl and throw things.

I'm dreading the middle grades for Phoebe, not because she isn't liked by her peers, but because I know how things can go south fast with girls and friendship at that age. I've already comforted her too many times because of a snub or a jab.

Once she invited a girl over to make Halloween lanterns out of milk jugs (I do have my Martha moments, though they may be few and far between). The girl happened to be chummy with another classmate who lived a few doors down and asked to go see this other girl. I said yes against my better judgement. Ten minutes later, my girl came back home, slamming the door and crying her eyes out. "Nina wants to stay at Bailey's!" she wailed.

I knew Nina wasn't being mean, nor was Bailey. I knew that both their moms, had they figured it out, would have not been okay with Nina ditching her playdate at our house. They were good girls, with nice moms, who hadn't meant to hurt anyone's feelings. But oh, it stung anyway. It was just one of those times when nobody meant to pull the trigger, but my child got grazed by a bullet anyway.

I do aspire to be sanely involved in my children's social conflicts, so I refrained from making a big deal out of it. (Actually, that's not entirely true. I do aspire to be sanely involved, but nothing makes me crazier than when my children, especially P, get picked on, bullied, slighted, and hurt in any way. Every mother that ever lived: You feel me. I know you do.)

Maybe it bugs me so much because now I get it. Alpha girls don't rise without our permission. When they don't get checked, their power runs amok. Viola, for one, got no pushback from me. I unquestioningly bowed down to her and her posse for all the good it did me. Actually, it harmed me, as it does anyone who has ever curtsied to a queen bee for no reason other than not wanting to get stung.

It seems to me it started in the locker room after gym or volleyball practice, early in our first year. As I was changing my clothes, I turned to see Viola staring at me and then slowly turning her head to whisper something to her friends. They all shot looks at me and then started giggling. As a unit, they turned their backs on me and left me alone with the smell of sweat and Love's Baby Soft.

I scrambled to get back in Viola's good graces. In the pencil-case episode, I crawled on hands and knees, flailing to stop the walls that were forming around me, forcing me out and pushing me down. And while nobody ever physically pushed me or shoved me up into the lockers and spit in my face, emotionally, my head was throbbing, and there was spit and mascara running down my cheek.

Viola was telling people I was a big, fat liar—which I was at the time. Looking back, I see that exaggerating was a way for me to try to curry favor from my peers. Lies appealed to me like candy, while the truth of who I was sat like a stone.

Not pretty enough.

Not cool enough.

Not lovable enough.

Not wanted enough.

Not enough.

Not.

Invisible.

I let the cracks do the talking then. There are cracks in everything, you know. We all have them upon birth. I happened to have an extra set, the fracture from the loss of my original family, the hurt that would kick up and give me trouble from time to time. Most people—especially adoptive parents—do not like to acknowledge the cracks. They don't want to think about the loss, because what exactly was lost? They picture their baby abandoned on a doorstep in China or languishing in an overstuffed orphanage in Ukraine. They imagine their child's birth parents—so messed up, drug-addled, and neglectful that the state had to step in and terminate parental rights. Even if the birth parents are good, decent folk who were simply not ready to have children, it's still hard to think of your child losing them. It's much easier to think about all they gained, which is you and a whole world of love and security.

Carissa Woodwyk, a Korean adoptee and therapist specializing in adoption, said it perfectly to a group of adoptive moms: "Because you get to love us, we have lost the people who were supposed to love us. We lose our original family . . . and this is deep in our bones."[1]

Deep in my bones, the cracks yawned and howled during those early junior-high months. I fantasized almost constantly about being rescued by my birth mother, even though the thought of finding her was terrifying. I've learned there has always been a pattern with me: Whenever my confidence and heart are at a low ebb, I wish and wonder the most about lost connections and what might have been. Being rejected by Viola—and henceforth the grade-eight powers that be—was like being kicked in a place already bruised.

They treated me as if I didn't exist—Christian private-school bullying at its finest, by the way—which reinforced my unlovableness with a boot to the shin. Plain old insecurity, which descends upon both those adopted and not adopted during junior high school, didn't help.

I've heard that loneliness is experienced in the same part of the brain as physical pain.[2] This is why breakups, rejections, and loss of any dear human connection hurt physically. Being bereft, left behind, and left aches for real.

I knew, in two languages, that God loved me. *Gott ist die Liebe, er liebt auch mich. Jesus loves me, this I know.* But that fact had yet to dig deep into my soul, as it would the following summer. Then I would take God's hand and invite Him to pull me up, to lift my head and heart and bind them to His. Then I would submit to grace and love like a waterfall. But that shining moment of transformation, at a youth conference on the campus of the University of Manitoba, was still almost a year away.

Mind you, I was dearly loved by my parents and grandparents. My grandma Loewen was an especially adoring presence. Though she spoke German and I spoke English, I could feel her love ringing through my life like a bell. But when you're thirteen or fourteen and your peers have rejected you, it feels like the whole world has turned against you. I was lost that year, a broken girl who felt so isolated, so far from being accepted and feeling acceptable.

Thankfully, there was no Internet. Also, I was just thirteen, still harbored by my conservative Mennonite upbringing, and I had no access whatsoever to any numbing substances. So I found comfort in three things:

- The music of 1981. "Too Much Time on My Hands" by Styx was the first record single I bought with my own money, and it was worth every penny. Also, listening to Blondie and Pat Benatar filled me up with girl power. Even though I was too feeble to hit anyone with my best shot, I wanted to.

- The Winnipeg Jets. Having been a card-carrying member of the Winnipeg Jets Junior Booster Club, I graduated to full-fledged crushes on Moe Mantha, Morris Lukowich, and Scott Arneil, in that order. My dad got Dan and me seven-dollar nosebleed seats to as many Jets games as he could afford, and we would gleefully watch the games and then wait around in the basement of the glorious old barn (the Winnipeg Arena, RIP) for the players' autographs. I lived for those postgame rink-rat episodes. The Arena, with its distinctive smell of ice and buttered popcorn and beer, was my domain, a true asylum for my orphan heart. Here I had access to my heroes (and crushes) that kids today could only dream about, and there was no sign of Viola Goossen anywhere. I idolized the Jets rain or shine, win or lose (they may have won nine games that year—out of eighty). I avidly attended games, watched them on TV, and listened to them on the radio that I kept next to my bed. My obsession iced my bumps and bruises, if you will, and gave me something to think about other than the latest snub at school.

- My kitten, Toby, who didn't care if everyone in grade eight thought I was a loser, only that I cuddled with him and occasionally came through on half a tin of tuna fish. Every ostracized human being should have a pet to get him or her through the day.

And of course my literary friend and role model was there for me while I was blacklisted at school. I found a friend in Anne's melodramatic speeches ("I am well in body although considerably rumpled up in spirit, thank you, ma'am"[3]), which gave voice to my pain. Her deep sensitivity to rejection and insult reflected my own. I clung to Anne, distracted by her hilarious capers and inspired to find hope and beauty in the cruelty of eighth grade. After all, Anne was able to put that insufferable hag, Josie Pye, in her place; maybe I could do the same with Viola. I didn't know it would get better, that it inevitably would blow over.

Josie Pye! How I long to travel back in time and flick you on the forehead, just once. There's nothing like a Pye Girl to bring out infantile instincts. When we consider literary mean girls, Josie is pretty high up on the list. She's no Nellie Oleson of *Little House on the Prairie* fame, mind you, but she's still pretty mean. Snooty as all get out, her uppity nose just a-sniffing for signs of weakness, Josie roams to and fro over her turf, seeking those whom she may devour.

Enter Anne Shirley, an orphan dressed in dowdy clothing so lacking by the current fashion standards of the schoolhouse that it was almost beneath Josie to take aim at this easy of a target.

Luckily for Josie, the foundling had red hair and freckles, as well as a proclivity for getting into scrapes, which provided plenty of currency for such a girl to trade on. Her feral instincts also told her that Anne Shirley was vulnerable. Mean girls can smell defenselessness a mile away.

Yet in the first duel to which we are privy, Anne came out on top, which gave me an inkling of hope that maybe I, too, could prevail one day. In Anne's case, it was the third week of the semester at the Avonlea school, which was "set back from the road and behind it was a dusky fir wood and a brook where all the children put their bottles of milk in the morning to keep cool and sweet until dinner hour."[4]

Our Anne had already scrabbled to near the top of the class, being whip smart and as hardworking as a lumberjack. The task at hand on this day: to go up to the blackboard and spell *ebullition*. (Ebullition: A no-show in my thesaurus, but upon further digging, I discovered it means "the action of bubbling or boiling," or "a sudden outburst of emotion or violence."[5] I think we can all agree that Maud knew this would be an important word in Anne's life.)

Anne spelled it like the champ that she was, catching Josie stealing a look in the spelling book and unseating her as the current head of the class in one fell swoop. (Where was Mr. Phillips, the teacher, when Josie Pye was cheating? He was mooning over Prissy Andrews, his sixteen-year-old student, because of course that was totally okay. Creeper.)

These schoolroom events were a boon to me in my time of need, and I'm sure a boon to anyone who has ever endured psychological intimidation. Our very own Anne of Green Gables swept Josie Pye of Pyeville "a look of freezing scorn."[6]

Yes, you heard it here: Anne shot her nemesis a laser of subzero disrespect. Josie's cheeks ignited. She rose from her desk and spelled *ebullition* wrong, despite her peek at the spelling book. She was rattled—and it was a win for Anne!

If only that were the end of the story. If only Josie Pye were not quite so *Pye,* a race, according to Mrs. Rachel Lynde, whose "mission in life was to keep schoolteachers reminded that earth isn't their home."[7] Anne may have won a battle, but the war raged on. In fact, Anne was almost killed in the midst of it.

I speak, naturally, of the Ridgepole Incident, when Josie taunt-ingly dared Anne to walk the horizontal beam along the edge of Mr. Barry's kitchen roof. Anne took the dare and then several steps before tumbling from roof to ground, shockingly un-killed but much injured in ankle and in spirit.

Anne's excuse was as lame as her leg: She couldn't stomach Josie Pye's scorn. "She would have crowed over me all my life,"[8] Anne wailed to a thoroughly unconvinced Marilla.

Throughout the entire book, Josie found that exposed spot in Anne's armor and skewered it. If we were to spin a medley of Josie's greatest hits, per se, it would sound like this:

- Sulky. (She moped when she didn't get the part of fairy queen in the school play.)

- Nasty. (She said that Julia Bell reminded her of a chicken jerking its head when Julia bowed to the audience before beginning to recite at a concert. Nice.)

- Gloating. (She giggled when beloved Miss Stacy caught Anne reading *Ben Hur* in class instead of reviewing Canadian history, a subject that, though I love my homeland everlastingly, can be as dry as peanut shells.)

- Undermining. (She tried shaking Anne's academic confidence at every turn. On one occasion she told Anne it was too bad her exam number was thirteen because "it's so unlucky."[9] And she took many, many more jabs.)

· Divisive. (She implied to Anne's old chum Diana that Anne would soon forget her, being *"infatuated"* with her new college friend Stella Maynard![10] Had she no shame?)

I save the worst thing for last: "Josie Pye says she is just going to college for education's sake, because she won't have to earn her own living; she says of course it is different with orphans who are living on charity—*they* have to hustle."[11]

This all compels me to speak in capital letters: WHAT IS WRONG WITH YOU, JOSIE PYE? Why don't you just shut your Pye hole, once and for all? All that plucking, poking, and stabbing, front and back! Was she raised by wolverines? (I will not compare her to a cat because that would be disrespectful toward cats. Plus, I don't want to risk my own cats shooting *me* looks of freezing scorn.)

Josie's digs must have picked at Anne's scabs something terrible, no matter how she tried to push back. Feisty as she was, Josie Pye often succeeded in getting under Anne's freckled skin. Proof: the famous scene when Anne tried to dye her hair raven black, only to stain it a striking hue of green. First, Anne hid under her covers in a puddle of shame and tears, her hair the color of mashed peas and carrots, only admitting her folly to Marilla when confronted. Then Anne was horrified when she discovered no amount of scrubbing would remove the green. Tearfully, Anne admitted that her fears were focused on the reaction of one person. "Oh, how Josie Pye will laugh! Marilla, I *cannot* face Josie Pye."[12]

When Anne returned to Avonlea School, looking like a shorn sheep after the green had been hacked from her hair, she was still able to hold her head high because only Diana knew the real story.

Naturally, Josie immediately hit Anne with a comparison to a "perfect scarecrow,"[13] but we see how Anne was growing, learning the value of letting things go—to a point. Ms. Pye Hole *was* subjected to another icy stare before Anne heaped hot coals upon her head and forgave her.

Anne's grace toward Josie is a thing of beauty. Other than a few frozen glares, Anne responded to Josie time after time by trying to forgive her and turn an enemy into a friend. When Josie took first prize at the provincial fair for her knitted lace, Anne felt glad, and gladder yet because she knew that this rejoicing was a sign of mercy and blessing upon her own soul.

Looking back on Anne's actions from my current perspective as the mother of a girl, I can see how much she has to teach both me and Phoebe about dealing with mean girls. She stood up to Josie when necessary with those looks of icy scorn and valiantly tried to see the good in her, despite little evidence of any goodness. Anne refused to get mired in the muddy waters of hating her enemy, an enemy who *did not stop* trying to belittle and shame her. Even when Anne had walked through the valley of the shadow, scooped hollow by loss, even then Josie made a crack about how Anne's hair looked redder than ever when she wore her black mourning clothes. No, the Josie Pyes of this world won't stop, unless someone stops them.

Anne, so saturated with feeling for her fellow hurt creature, somehow knew that there was a reason Josie Pye acted the way she did. She reminds me to ask myself, *How have the Josie Pyes of the world been hurt, so they in turn hurt others, maybe even me and mine?*

During my own lonely period in eighth grade, I paid close attention to how Anne responded to Josie. How I wish I had had the starch back then to shoot even one look of freezing scorn at my foes! Instead, I bent from my brokenness, pulled to the ground and trampled.

If I could go back in time to pay a visit to Josie Pye, I'd make a stopover in 1981. I'd park my blue Doctor Who TARDIS in the lot of my alma mater, and I'd make my way to the dungeon, just after stopping in the cafeteria for Mrs. King and Mrs. Dick's chocolate chip cake. I'd tell them that their cake is an unsurpassed masterpiece of pastry perfection and give hugs all around.

Once I found the girl I was, I'd hold her in my arms for a long time. I would tell her she is loved more than she knows and worth more than gold. My words might sound like this:

Hang on, it'll all blow over soon. There, there. It does get better. You wouldn't believe it if I told you, but someday soon you are going to have the best friends in the whole wide world, friends who make you laugh and who value you and your gifts to this world. You're even going to give your mother a heart attack when you insist on ten bridesmaids at your wedding! And Viola is one of them (just kidding)! But seriously, look around you. A few of your lifelong friends are in this very room, believe it or not. You feel like you are too sensitive, but oh—how the world needs feelers. How this dented old world needs people to notice things, to offer compassion and tears and kindness! How the broken road is consecrated because it leads cracked people like us to Jehovah Rapha, the God who heals. There is a crack in everyone—that's how the light gets in.

When Viola Goossen drops her pencil case, gently but firmly hold yourself back. Let Viola get it. Don't bend. Throw your shoulders back and be bold, be strong—not because you are those things, but because God is with you. Don't bend. You are weak, but He is strong. Stop lying, especially to yourself. It tastes like candy, but it's really poisonous. The truth nourishes and makes things whole. God will help you forgive Viola and see her through His eyes. You'll never be friends, exactly, again, but in time, you will remember her as she was to you once, your fun, laughing pal. You'll forgive her and wish her only love and good things. You'll come to realize that Viola didn't know how much her actions hurt you; she, like everyone else, was dealing with her own cracked places. And when you figure that last part out, it will change everything.

As Mrs. Lynde remarked, this earth is not our home. In this life, we will always have the Josie Pyes with us, the hurt ones who hurt us.

This earth is not our home—it gives me hope and a fresh yearning for a someday world with no more cracks, only wholeness, in a place lit by God Himself, where the light infuses everything and everybody. When this life is over, this is what I long for: that two old friends will clasp hands, sing songs, and laugh again by an unimaginable Lake of Shining Waters, rejoicing because the lion and the lamb have lain down together at last.

·4·

A Kindred Spirit

The book of welcome says, Let people see you. . . . It's called having friends,
choosing each other, getting found, being fished out of the rubble. It blows you
away how this wonderful event happened—me in your life, you in mine.

ANNE LAMOTT, *SMALL VICTORIES*

FROM THE START, there was nothing fearful about Clara Wiebe. None of this timid, new-girl posture for her. She was six feet tall, with curly, dirty-blonde hair and huge army-green eyes. She bobbed into our eighth-grade English class, her long strides and bouncy way of getting around noticeably different from anyone else. She grinned and gave a goofy, hectic little wave after the teacher notified us that Clara had just moved here with her family from the rural town of Steinbach. I thought she was weird from the start, but good weird, definitely good weird. "Take me or leave me; I really don't care"— that's what her stance told me about her.

The Beautiful People took her in with a glance and left her alone, neither fawning over her as fresh blood or picking on her. Clara's kind of beauty—towering, dramatic, unusual—held little appeal for fourteen-year-old girls who thought the epitome of exquisiteness was to be five feet tall and ninety-nine pounds, soaking wet. She was no threat.

Denelle Loepkke, the preacher's daughter, had laid some claim to Clara already, as their parents knew one another somehow. Of all the girls at school, Denelle was maybe the most innocent in my shunning. We know now there are queen bees and targets, but the vast majority of girls are simply bystanders, who don't join in the shabby treatment of targets or do anything to stop it. Denelle was a kindhearted bystander and behaved toward me as if I were a person, not a nonentity. I returned the favor by swiping Clara from under her nose, something I still wish had gone down differently.

But then again, how else could it have gone down? It's like the couple who is just starting to date. Everything is positive and promising, when suddenly the guy introduces his new girl to his roommate, and as it turns out, the roommate and the new girl are soul mates, and the first guy emcees their wedding with a sheepish look on his face. There was no way this friendship between Clara and me was not going to happen.

Denelle, out of the goodness of her heart, and maybe with some pressure from her parents, included me in a weekend afternoon of cake decorating at her house. I was ecstatic. Clara was deep into a food-coloring creation by the time I got there. Her face and hair were smeared with Smurf-blue icing, giving her a zombie look. I don't remember what we laughed about, but soon I was laughing so hard I was crying and gagging. Those laughs went down like medicine, a tonic for what ailed me. Clara was the funniest person I had ever met, and I could tell she didn't give a flying fig for what Viola Goossen or anyone else thought of her. If I even brought up Viola's name, Clara's eyes would roll. "Who cares about her?" she would say. And then she would change the subject, as if the Violas of this world were crashing bores, not worth discussing. That was the cure I needed most.

So I straightened up without knowing, and I stopped bowing and scraping for the approval of my peers. I had Clara now, and she understood and accepted me. We drove our mothers to distraction with all the requests to be together, to monopolize the family phone with hour-long calls after spending all day together at school. At my house, Clara and I would wait until everyone was asleep and then raid the freezer, chewing on half-frozen brownies on the Murphy bed in our basement, watching music videos hosted by Terry David Mulligan on channel 2. Clara made me feel as if I belonged again.

At Clara's place, we would lie awake for hours, talking and stifling giggles amid the chatter of her crazy bird, Louie Kablouie, and the blobby glow of her red lava lamp. Above us hung about twenty McDonald's french fry boxes on strings, an art installation by Clara. The first time I came over, she showed me her painting *Blood and Sunshine*, a canvas splashed with dried drips of red and yellow paint. For a girl like me, who favored Monet and Renoir, *Blood and Sunshine* was a stretch, but it fit Clara's subversive MO to perfection.

If I was Anne, all dramatic speeches, flowery imagination, and a heart noticeably worn on the sleeve of my pink angora sweater, Clara walked in the clogs of another carrot-topped orphan: Pippi Longstocking. Though Clara did not have a father who was a castaway king on some South Seas island, she was a firm iconoclast—in dress (mostly black with emerald green thrown in ornamentally), hair style (at one point half buzzed), and the ability to neutralize bullies with one hand tied behind her back. Her superpowers, like Pippi's, were intense loyalty and Teflon skin.

With Clara as my shelter and touchstone, I could have strapped myself very comfortably into the role as her sidekick, riding shotgun until we graduated in four years. But then her dad got a job as a minister of music at a church in British Columbia, and I lost her just a year and a half after I had found her. We were crushed, to say the least. Soon after she imparted this horrendous news at the snowy bus stop, my dad got us tickets to go see Amy Grant, whom I held in the deepest of awe. (My room, filled with posters and other merchandising materials from my dad's Christian bookstore was like Six-Flags-Over-Amy. The only thing missing was a wax Amy, although I did have a cardboard cutout Amy, which was probably stalkerish enough.) Her opening act was Michael W. Something, a frenetic piano player who zigzagged around the stage like a laser beam. Normally, we would have impatiently bided our time for Amy to take the stage, but when he broke into "Friends," Clara and I clutched hands and sobbed bitter tears. The song, inspired by friends of the songwriter's who had moved, hit us square between the eyes. How would we ever survive high school without our other half?

When Clara left, late in the summer before tenth grade, it wrenched and ripped us both. Letters flew back and forth over the prairies to Vancouver, along with mixtapes comprised of music by the Eurythmics and Duran Duran, plus hours of haphazard ramblings about boys, using baby powder as dry shampoo, boys, Madonna, and boys. This was in the days of long-distance rates, and both of us were in almost perpetual hot water from our poor parents about their skyrocketing phone bills. Without the shelter of each other, cold drafts of loneliness beset us both, and we were orphaned in a different way—bereft, left behind, and left. Clara shaved her head and began kohl-rimming her green eyes. I moped around the house and ate vast quantities of half-frozen brownies. We lived for New Year's Eve, when we would be reunited in Banff, Alberta, at the Mennonite Brethren national youth conference.

Yet I realized something a few weeks into the new, forlorn school year. I went into tenth grade as a loner, planning to keep to myself, as my heart had traveled with irreplaceable Clara to Vancouver. But I carried her influence with me and was changed. I was tougher, more hard-wearing in the face of fifteen-year-old girl drama. Even though my dearest friend was one thousand miles away, she had imparted some of her nonstick coating to me. Not only that, but I also now had my faith in which to dwell. Teresa of Avila described God's home in our hearts as the "interior castle," and it made all the difference to me to be able to go to the castle and talk things over with the King.

Even so, it came as a great surprise that fall that I could laugh and commiserate with other girls and even form real bonds with a few of them, bonds that last to this day. I discovered I could stand on my own two feet without Clara; I was so much more than just a sidekick.

But, oh, how I needed Clara Wiebe to bob into my English class that day in eighth grade. How we *all* need a like-minded soul to come along at just the right time to rescue us, to remind us of our own capacity to love and to stand.

Experiencing true friendship after a poverty of loneliness is like suddenly having access to the treasure chest in Pippi's Villa Villekulla. Each phone call and shared meal and visit is like a golden coin, a pearl of great price. A friend can be your own version of a parted sea, of manna from a loving hand. Each time you are understood and accepted, your jokes laughed at and your sorrows made smaller by care, you feel richer than Pippi and so very lucky.

As for Anne, who had lived such a famished, loveless existence before arriving on Prince Edward Island (PEI), she needed Diana Barry even more than most of us need our kindred spirits. Because when your previous best friend is one who exists only in a glass reflection, smashed and cracked by your drunken foster father, you feel all the more rich and lucky when your bosom friend comes along.

...

I adore the beginnings of Anne Shirley and Diana Barry's friendship, when Anne trembled in excitement and fear as she prepared to join

Marilla on an errand to Orchard Slope to meet Diana, her potential friend. As readers, we anticipate what extraordinary event will happen in Barry's Garden, and we cheer her on.

Did Anne somehow know that in Diana she would find the acceptance her shriveled little heart longed for? Did she have an instinct that her loneliness and grief would melt away in the company of someone who accepted her exactly as she was?

She could wait no longer for a true friend. Amid the crimson roses, bleeding hearts, peonies, and white narcissi of the Barry garden, Anne just came out with it:

> *"Oh, Diana," ... clasping her hands and speaking almost in a whisper, "do you think—oh, do you think you can like me a little—enough to be my bosom friend?"*[1]

Diana laughed, because here was a funny girl with a funny way of putting things. And Maud lets us know that "Diana always laughed before she spoke."[2] But Diana liked this way. She saw at once that Anne was weird, but good weird. "A queer girl,"[3] Diana called her, as in atypical, peculiar, and unlike anyone Diana had ever met before. Through friendly eyes, Anne's "spirit, fire, and dew" translated to something more like "vivid, unconventional, and lovable."

Anne and Diana's friendship was larger than life, one for the books. Anne was left behind no more: She had found her best friend, her first partner in life.

Diana taught Anne to sing "Nelly in the Hazel Dell," a song to shell peas by. Clara taught me to enjoy the music of U2, Howard Jones, and Duran Duran, even though I didn't name my firstborn son Simon Le Bon Craker after all.

Diana told Anne that Charlie Sloane was *"dead gone"*[4] on her, while Clara sent me a rose one lackluster Valentine's Day with a card reading, "I want you. Richard Gere," which is the closest I'll ever get to hearing that Richard Gere is *dead gone* on me.

Diana's sympathetic gaze counteracted Josie Pye's malicious one, and she turned "pale with pity"[5] when her friend was wrongfully punished by Mr. Phillips.

Anne and Diana were perfect for each other. While Diana was a placid pond, Anne seethed like the ocean with waves of joy and pain, even to the point of conjuring despair at the thought of being parted from her friend.

She imagined Diana getting married someday, adorned in snow-white garments; a black-eyed, rosy-cheeked, raven-curled queen. She cast herself as Suffering Bridesmaid—yes, in puffy sleeves at long last but with a cracking heart beneath her brave martyr's smile.[6] She hated Diana's future husband passionately, to the point where I fear she might have done harm to good, docile Fred Wright had his future identity as Diana's groom been revealed to Anne in that moment. (Run, Fred, run!)

Of course they made mistakes together, and a few of them were doozies, such as the episode I like to call "Pouncing on Aunt Josephine." It all started when Diana invited Anne to a concert at the Debating Club and overnight accommodations in the spare room at her parents' home, at which point Anne ascended to the ceiling like an orange-dipped balloon. For Anne, each "thrill was thrillier than the last," even that of Mr. Phillips giving Mark Antony's oration over Caesar's dead body and gawking at Prissy Andrews as he finished every sentence.[7]

(I'd like a wee word with Prissy's parents, the Avonlea school board, and Mr. Creeper Phillips himself. Yes, we are told by scholars of the era that Mr. Phillips's interest in his sixteen-year-old student was actually well within the bounds of propriety for the time, that even the fact that he wrote poems "to Priscilla" during class time and was often caught ogling her with big, simpering, watery cow eyes, was considered appropriate behavior then. Are we to be comforted by this? I think not. Maud may have based Mr. Phillips upon Mr. Mustard, a teacher who proposed marriage to her when she was sixteen and living with her father in Saskatchewan.[8] I'd like a word with them as well—Mr. Mustard and Mr. Montgomery! By the way, I added "watery" and "cow eyes" out of my own imagination.)

Back to Anne at the Debate Club recital: She was changed forever by this experience, and ironically, by the mistake to come that very night. If the dazzling recital hadn't been enough excitement, Anne was about to spend the night in the Barrys' spare room, her fondest wish. A home's most luxurious accommodations were generally found in their guest rooms. As Anne told Marilla, "Think of the honor of your little Anne being put in the spare room bed."[9] Anne Shirley, orphan, was finally worthy of someone's softest and most luxurious apple leaf quilt, their peak picturesque views, their best pristine mirror and polished dressing table. Even anticipating it made her feel like a million bucks.

Once Anne and Diana had their white nightgowns on, they raced each other down the hall, through the spare room door, and sprang upon the bed and a slumbering Aunt Josephine like two gigantic grasshoppers.

We all know it was Aunt Josephine's fault for showing up too early.

Be that as it may, Anne owned her mistake and did what she did best, which was to win people over. Disarming Aunt Josephine was perhaps the biggest win in Anne's career and led to another life-bringing friendship. Becoming friends with Aunt Josephine taught Anne that affinity sometimes occurs in unlikely sources and that devoted pals are not as rare as she once thought.

Anne said it: "Tomorrow is a new day with no mistakes in it yet,"[10] and I'm betting these two gal pals never again sprang into a spare room bed without first checking for rich, crabby relatives beneath the covers.

But, ah, there's just something about mistakes with friends, getting into scrapes together that probably wouldn't have happened if left to our own devices.

I think of my friend Bonnie and me, overcome by a fit of giggles during our clarinet duet at the Pioneer Girls mother-daughter banquet, our giggles causing the dulcet tones of our horns to come out in bursts of bagpipe-y squeaks. Nobody was blessed by that musical package.

I consider my friend Nancy's and my near-fatal road trip from Chicago, where we were both attending college, to Winnipeg. Nancy had been pickpocketed at Water Tower Mall, so her five hundred dollars in cash was gone, including the two hundred dollars my parents had given her for my portion of the trip home. We had no cash for our trip and no credit cards, either. With the optimism of youth, we set out anyway and drove right into the teeth of a blizzard, at one point spinning out on the highway and screaming our lungs out. The angels were prudently occupied by our haphazardness that day, and we arrived in one piece at a motel in Minneapolis, where Nancy's alternator promptly died. Safe but cash poor and stranded, we lived on "chicken noodle" soup—aka "bouillon"—out of the vending machine for two days while a mechanic fixed the little blue Civic.

Or there was the time in college when my beautiful roommate Becky accepted a date to eat in the school cafeteria with a fellow whose personality was sorely lacking in snap, crackle, and pop. Sweet Becky couldn't say no, and neither could I when she begged me to come along and chaperone. Was it the cod loin on offer in the cafeteria that day that set me off, or was it Myron Flikkema's robotic way of talking? I was once again capsized with giggles, a theme in my life. Poor Myron kept trying to get something going with Becky over plates of cod loin; he might as well have tried to start a fire by rubbing two wet twigs together. I continued to hoot like an impaired owl, which gave Becky something to say to Myron: "She's not right in the head. I'm so sorry," over and over again.

Sure, we didn't learn that much from our mistakes, my friends and I, other than that it's a bad idea to drive in blizzards and chaperone your roommate on a date she never should have accepted, but, hey! That's what memories are made of.

...

While revisiting the series, I noticed for the first time that there was one way in which Anne and Diana did not relate completely to each other: Anne's writing. Diana was many things—loyal, even-tempered, and mostly sensible—but a writer she was not. Diana admired Anne's writing talents to the skies, but that's not the same thing as being a companion on "the Alpine path," as Maud called her own writing career.[11] Still, Diana was always game for whatever monkeyshines Anne suggested, even joining, with Jane and Ruby, the story club to "cultivate" her imagination.[12]

> *"It's extremely interesting," Anne told Marilla. "Each girl has to read her story out loud and then we talk it over. We are going to keep them all sacredly and have them to read to our descendants."*[13]

It was Anne's first writing community, something Maud never really had in her own life. Except for her pen pals Ephraim Weber, a Mennonite writer, and George Boyd MacMillan, a Scottish journalist, she had no one with whom to climb the Alpine path. Worse, she never had anyone to catch her when she fell off that jagged, mountainous trail with bloody knees and a sick, discouraged heart, like every writer before or since.

Her lack makes me all the more grateful for my own story club, The Guild. As Mrs. Rachel Lynde would say, it was perfectly providential how we seven scribblers came together. A local reporter named Ann and I both were jumbo with child—my middle, her youngest—when she interviewed me about my first book, a little baby name tome. We hit it off, and she suggested we start a writing group with a couple of other local scribes. Two of us became five and then nine and then seven, the final number we've settled on after a few partings and moves out of town.

We've shared it all in The Guild: aging parents; grief; teenagers; risk taking (Shelly urged Tracy to be bold, fly to Cyprus, and jump from a boat into the Mediterranean for character research on the biblical Jonah, which she *did*); and what to do when an arsonist burns down your house (When Alison's house was torched by a lunatic, the first thing we did was show up at her sister-in-law's with an emergency kit, including chocolate sea foam, a lovely card, a Guild T-shirt, and a boxful of books. Then we all cried our eyes out from relief, shock, and love.).

Together we and our works have encountered screaming success and long, cold silences that feel a lot like failure. We are each other's Sherpa guides as we mountaineer Maud's path, a trail pitted with high peaks and deep, rutted valleys. We are for each other when an editor says no, when an agent says maybe and then vanishes into space, when a novel one of us has written with so much tender care is praised by critics and roundly passed over by book buyers. We have met once a month for years at Schuler Books and Music in Grand Rapids, unless it's our Christmas Tea (Tracy's cheese pie is not to be missed), the writer's conference we founded together each October, or the occasional sleepover featuring a quantity of chocolate sea foam and a movie starring Colin Firth in knee-length pants.

This last summer, one of us experienced a piercing disappointment; a "sure thing" had become "not a chance" in the head-spinning fashion for which the publishing industry is known. We rose up as one big fireball of indignation and wrath. Tracy, who has a fondness for speaking in military terms, led the charge. "First rule of combat?" she wrote in an e-mail minutes after hearing about our member's rejection, "Keep moving when fired upon. And we've got your back, because we all have scorch marks. Trust the ones with the scorch marks."

I trust the ones with the scorch marks, every single one a wounded healer, each a contributor to my life's story. Without all my friends, writers and nonwriters, I would be curled in the fetal position somewhere, sucking my thumb.

I'm going to go out on a limb here and say that for the orphan's heart, friendship means even more. Our beginnings were marked by the loss of people vital to us, so when we are intentionally picked and preferred by friends, it's kind of a big deal. I witness Phoebe with her friends—playing soccer, caring tenderly for animals, bombing around on their bikes—and I smile. She is known and cared for by her friends in a different, essential way. She belongs to them and they to her.

Bosom friends are like this: We chose each other and were found. We fished each other out of the rubble. It blows me away how this wonderful event happened—her in my life, she in mine.

Bonnie, the most like Diana Barry of all my friends, is unflappable, kind, and true. She is stuck with me as long as the sun and moon endure.

Nancy followed the same path as I from Mennonite Winnipeg girl to Chicago, the city of broad shoulders. We each married exotic foreign men—one from Michigan, the other from Florida—and are teaching our American children about the True North we love. Nancy was there for me more than any other friend when my dad was dying and then gone. I love her like a sister.

Becky has a heart as big as a house, serves grace on a platter, and has been my confidante and partner in countless emotional treks. She is incapable of judging, which makes me want to let her see me, as is.

Lori, my first friend, is now the angel on my shoulder. She feels kindred and present, even still. We shared a name and a street; our league of two was forged the day she stayed behind with me in kindergarten, when she quickly tied my hat strings into a bow. The teacher had kept me back, appalled that I didn't know how to tie a bow yet without looking at it. Lori was appalled that the teacher was such a crank. We walked home together hand in hand that day and many days after that.

Though our closeness tapered off during the years that we attended different middle schools and high schools, I never failed to feel comforted and rooted—*aligned*—somehow when passing her house, six houses from mine. Lori was still there, my old companion and ally, along with her family. Gravelly voiced Mrs. McCaskill had been a second mother to me, driving us to hockey games, feeding me Pizza Pops, and chatting with us as she baked in the sun, slathered in baby oil and wearing a gold lamé bikini. This low-coverage ensemble stood in stark contrast to my own mum's modest bathing attire. (She would not have worn gold lamé even in a one-piece suit with a skirt attached, because we all know gold lamé might lead to disco dancing.) Mrs. McCaskill taught me that there is no correlation between bathing suit choices and the ability to nurture, no appropriate costume for maternal instincts. She always referred to me as her kid.

I didn't know how attached I was to this family and their girl until

I got the letter from my mum at Camp Arnes, where I worked as a camp counselor the summer after graduating from high school: Lori had been diagnosed with a rare soft tissue cancer. We were both eighteen years old. I shivered there on the hot bench by the canteen and wrapped my arms around myself to keep from breaking. *How could it be?*

Thirteen years later, I held Lori's hand as she was dying and held back a river of tears through superhuman effort. Lori had survived five malignancies since her initial diagnosis; she would not survive the sixth. She wanted to talk about leaving this blue marble of our earth and what was to come for her. Her parents were not religious people; neither were her closest friends or her husband. Astonishingly, she remembered things taught in the backyard Bible club at my house an eon before, during the days of Popsicles and tire swings, things seeded by the Holy Ghost Himself and watered by a thousand prayers. She wanted to take Jesus' hand and trust Him to save her and keep her. One of the greatest honors of my life was leading her to that pierced hand that provides all of our healing. Soon He would take her to the place He had prepared for her. Soon, she would be gone, but not lost.

On our last day together, I smiled through blurry eyes (oh, it was hard!) and talked to Lori about heaven. *Look homeward, angel. Look! You'll be there soon, and I will carry you here with me until we meet on that beautiful shore.* Every day since, I have looked at the brilliant blue stone on my right hand—her sapphire class ring—and I remember. I remember my first partner in life. And I think again that death steals so much, but it articulates a friendship like nothing else.

...

And what became of Clara, my bosom friend who freed me from slavery to the opinions of my own Josie Pye? She up and ran off with Fred Wright, er, Bruno Klassen, a fellow U2 fan from our high school.

The bride wore ivory, and the Suffering Maid of Honour wore dark green velvet as she made a funny little speech.

This has taken me a long time to parse: Best friends may be inseparable for a season before the road diverges geographically, politically, or spiritually. Your best friend takes one road, and you take another. There is a day that comes that is very hard—when you know that something funny will happen to her on the way to class, and she'll tell only one person about it and that'll be Bruno, not you. Maybe that's my orphan heart talking, but it takes only about twenty years of wishing for things to be the same before you realize that it is okay, really, it is, that they will never be.

When best friendships change, you make room for new types of relationships, and you wake up one day and realize you couldn't live without having had those post-BF friends. They have added so much. If things had stayed the same with Clara, there wouldn't have been room for Bonnie, Becky, Nancy, and other loves of my life. I'm so glad there was room.

Clara and I are still friends, of course, although we rarely see each other. Recently, we all miraculously ended up in Chicago on the same night, though Clara and Bruno live in Ontario and my husband and I live in Michigan. We had a ball, eating Lou Malnati's deep-dish pizza, strolling Rush Street, and catching up and laughing. Clara and I could still speak in shorthand with each other. The surprise get-together made me grateful anew for our era, mine and hers, how it formed and ennobled me, and made me who I am. Plus, that Bruno Klassen is a pretty swell guy after all.

Anne's divergent road also led her away from Diana, to new friends such as Phil, Stella, and Leslie, compatible souls to share her college experience, teaching life, and motherhood. Yet Diana was waiting in Avonlea, Anne's touchstone always.

Few of us will ever experience that kind of undying closeness, but then again, few of us will ever need a friend the way Anne needed Diana, her salve and saving grace.

Yet if Anne teaches us anything about friendship, it's that the spark of resemblance—you spotting me, me spotting you—can exist even in the strangest and most unexpected places. In the final analysis, it's nothing but splendid to discover there are so many kindred spirits in this world.

He Shouldn't Have Called Her "Carrots," But Oh, That Gilbert Blythe!

The course of true love never did run smooth.

WILLIAM SHAKESPEARE, *A MIDSUMMER NIGHT'S DREAM*

IT WAS A SNOW DAY, and Phoebe, eight, was downstairs watching the luminous *Anne of Green Gables* miniseries on DVD. (The first eight hours are luminous. As for the add-on movies, completely unrelated to the books, I pretend the Anne and Gilbert actors are instead part of a World War I movie.) Suddenly, I heard Phoebe pounding up the stairs to my office. She burst through the door, eyes wide with alarm.

"Mom! Something tragic has happened! Gilbert Blythe is *dying*, and he's engaged to someone else—*not* Anne!"

I restrained myself from explaining that Gilbert is never engaged to anyone but Anne in the books, that Anne just thinks he is, and then I agreed—this was the height of tragedy. "Just keep watching," I said, giving her a squeeze. "You never know how things are going to turn out."

Phoebe loves Gilbert Blythe because, well, who wouldn't? Also, her very favorite part of the whole story is the slate incident. Phoebe's idea of a good time would definitely be smashing slates over the heads of her classmates Owen Silasma, Nolan Kaiser, and their ilk. She laughs hysterically every time that slate comes down on Gil's cute head.

Ah, Gilbert Blythe . . . How about a collective swoon for the guy who was so into our Anne he took the blame when *she* tried to give *him* a concussion? *Sigh.* Who doesn't have a literary crush on Gilbert Blythe? I don't see a lot of hands raised. So great was his devotion and gallantry to Anne of Green Gables, I submit to you that Gilbert is the leading man to end leading men. Just a boy next door, you say? Yes and no. It's his quiet smoldering—for years—that elevates this boy next door to crush-worthy.

Sure, there's always Mr. Darcy, all suppressed passion behind an aloof exterior. Yes, in England there *is* a statue of him emerging from water, wearing a white shirt and seething wildly. By all means, Mr. Darcy possesses that unapproachable-yet-simmering-with-unbridled-passion aura that most women find irresistible. But take away the mists and the moors, and what do you have? A cranky man in short pants, that's what!

There's also Manly Wilder. To be fair, many bookworm girls *have* developed an infatuation for Almanzo Wilder, he of the log-sawing biceps and heated looks at Laura Ingalls across snow-covered prairie sleighs. Certainly Almanzo is a valid storybook squeeze. After all, he did risk his life to save the pioneers (including Laura's family) of De Smet, South Dakota, from starvation during the hard winter of 1881. Really, he had most of us at "Hello, my name is Almanzo [for some strange reason], but you, l'il lady? You can call me Manly."

Yet next to our guy Gil, even the mannish Manly is reduced to so much *Farmer Boy* eye candy.

Those two heartthrobs of the written word, Fitzwilliam Darcy and Almanzo Wilder, pined for their Lizzie and their Laura for what—months? Their pining cannot hold a candle to the constancy, the steadfastness, the inextinguishable flame of yearning that burned in Gilbert's heart for Anne Shirley for those many years.

This is why one can buy pillows with Gilbert's face on them,[1] or rather, the face of Jonathan Crombie, the actor who played Gilbert in the movie.

Jonathan Crombie . . . he was gone too soon. When news of his death broke in mid-April 2015, the outpouring of love for this actor and the character he brought to vivid, yearning life brought me to tears. He made manifest the Gilbert of our imaginations so that it was impossible to read the books again (and again) without picturing him as Anne's one and only. He brought Anne's kindred mate to life with sparks, grace, and depth.

The response to Crombie's death underscored for me the enormous affection millions of us have, not only for Anne, but for Matthew, Marilla, Mrs. Rachel, Diana—and especially for Gilbert. It made me ache to see #GilbertBlythe trending on social media, and then I felt stung again when he *wasn't* trending just two days later. People had moved on, so quickly. Yet I knew that the global expression of grief and love had not been a fluke. Crombie's death reminded readers of Gilbert's place in their hearts, as an old friend and a first love. It reminded us that we all want to be loved as Gil loved Anne, to be noticed and adored for exactly who we are—pungent hair color, quirks, flaws, and all. One of my friends, Alexandra, put it so beautifully: "Gilbert taught me how love felt. As I watched him on screen and read *all* of the books over and over as a girl, I wanted what he and Anne had: chemistry, devotion and mutual respect."[2]

I think that helps explain why, even before Crombie's death, there were manifestations of our collective adoration for Gil, such as pillows, and Gilbert Toffee, which I bought, though I don't even care for toffee. There are knitting patterns for Gilbert-style, vaguely Edwardian scarves. There are musical montages on YouTube featuring tender scenes of Anne and Gilbert set to the ballads of Air Supply and other great bands of our time. It's a wonder to me that Gilbert cologne has not been developed, sold, and sprayed on the menfolk of Anne fans everywhere.

This is why I like to do dishes alone to the strains of *Anne and Gilbert*, the soundtrack to the perfectly luscious new musical that debuted in Charlottetown in 2013. (I say "alone" because my husband does not sufficiently appreciate musical theater; though, as he points out, he has watched all eight legitimate hours of the *Anne of Green Gables* movie and listened to both the first and fifth books of the book series on tape, so surely he *cannot be expected* to also enjoy bouncy show tunes about Gilbert Blythe. In deference to a long and successful marriage, I do grant him this point.) The first song is entitled "Mr. Blythe," and it is an homage to Avonlea's cutest new schoolteacher (and a whopping improvement over Mr. Phillips, *that's what*).

Every human being who draws breath should go see *Anne and Gilbert*, mind you, but in case that's not an option just this minute, here is a snippet of the soundtrack's first tune: "Mr. Blythe! You're not just *bee-auuut-iful* . . . Mr. Blythe! You're not just wonderful to *seeeee*."[3] It evolves (Doyle would say "devolves") from there into ever more rapturous statements of giddiness, gaiety, and potential fainting.

Well, it's about time someone wrote a song about Gilbert Blythe, winker of inexpressible drollery, foeman worthy of Anne's steel, and prompter of quick, queer little beats in the hearts of us all.

"Carrots!"

Oh, Gilbert, I'm begging you—don't say it! You've been getting away with calling dark-haired Diana "Crow" for years, but this lassie is unlike any you've teased before.

I just wish there were a way to book travel and warn G. Blythe that it will be an ill wind that blows in the aftermath of comparing this girl's hair to that harvest vegetable. It will blow for years, and it will blow at minus thirty degrees with the wind chill factor. It will blow so cold, his very shadow will freeze to the ground. But he's going to do what he's going to do.

One of my chief pleasures in reentering Anne's story when writing this book was to experience again the delicious flutters and tizzies of her romance with Gilbert. The flirting, the longing, the attraction, the almost endless wait for emotional payoff, the sparks! It's all just so *delectable*! As a grown woman, I found I had a whole new appreciation for Gilbert's devotion for his girl. *We* know she is worthy, deep down, but Gooseberry Girl sure doesn't *behave* in a worthy manner for what seems like a stone age.

But it's Gilbert who behaved badly, shortly after they laid eyes on each other for the first time. Mere moments after their meeting, Gilbert winked at Anne with a look so dense with drollery we are told it is "inexpressible."[4] Unfortunately, Anne did not find this wink funny or within the bounds of good manners.

You know what they say about first impressions.

But it was not until the afternoon that things really began to happen.

Had Gilbert Blythe known what he knew just moments later, he would never, ever have uttered the words *he thought* were mildly teasing and flirty but were actually appallingly flammable. But you don't know what you don't know.

> *Gilbert reached across the aisle, picked up the end of Anne's long red braid, held it out at arm's length, and said in a piercing whisper, "Carrots! Carrots!"*[5]

Anne responded immediately, springing from her seat, calling him names, and *crrrrr--aaaaacking* her slate over his head with a booming thwack. That had to hurt—both his ego and his head.

Mr. Phillips, that paragon of pedagogy, punished Anne for her behavior, at which point Gilbert Blythe showed us a hint of the absolute mensch he was to become. He spoke up "stoutly"[6]—nothing wishy-washy about our Gil—taking the blame for Anne's explosive act. *It was really my fault. I provoked her . . .*

Of course, this did nothing to soften Anne's rage. Nor did Gilbert's apology, filled with remorse, ending with "Don't be mad for keeps, now."[7] Nor his feeble attempts at flirting a little later on, when Anne was forced to sit next to him in class. *Gil, did you really think a pink candy heart stamped with "You are sweet" would make everything hunky-dory once again?*

Her comeback is deluxe: "Whereupon Anne arose, took the pink heart gingerly between the tips of her fingers, dropped it on the floor, ground it to powder beneath her heel, and resumed her position without deigning to bestow a glance on Gilbert."[8]

Clearly, Gilbert was struggling, trying to restore order to his cute-boy universe. But throwing a pink candy heart at the problem was like trying to put out a fire by spitting on it.

You're in for it now, buddy. We know you didn't mean a thing by that "Carrots" comment, but you've hurt her feelings excruciatingly, and now you will be ground to powder beneath her feet. The iron has entered her soul! Anne was mad for keeps, and then some.

. . .

Reopening Anne and Gilbert's story also brought to mind memories of my own beginnings with the love of my life, an overused term but one that fits. Like Gilbert, my love was no flash in the pan, though it started with an unexpected flash of attraction, a wink of allure over a cafeteria table. Before finding the one, there were a number of others, boys whom I thought at the time would complete me and fill forever my orphan heart's hunger pangs. What I didn't know then was that even after you've found the one, a good and steady love, only a Father's love, only the Bread of Life, can really make you full. Only a Father's love can make you belong.

Nobody thought it would last between Doyle and me. We had come to our urban college from two very different worlds. He was a country boy through and through, down to his fringed mountain-man moccasins and his woolly beard. He was quiet, steady, and calm. On the other hand, I relished living in a high-rise apartment in downtown Chicago—the smells of gyros and the chocolate factory, the sounds of sirens, "Taxi!", and a never-ending strum and twang of humanity. He was Jeremiah Johnson, far from his wilderness, weary of civilization, and I was Mary Tyler Moore throwing my hat in the air in the city I adored. I was giggly, a talker, on the social activities committee at school. He sang bass in the men's chorus and played his guitar up on high in Culbertson Hall. Doyle and Lorilee did not make sense on paper. But oh—those flickering blue eyes and those gleaming white teeth.

It was 1990, and I paraded around campus like a giant American Girl doll in my puffed sleeves and raging floral patterns. One day at dinner, someone made the not untrue remark that I looked like a sofa. "Doyle, do you think I look like a sofa?" I fluttered.

"Nope," he said, flashing pearly whites and winking at me with what might be construed as inexpressible drollery. "Sofas are horizontal."

The bluest eyes, the whitest teeth, and drollery, too? It was all over for me. Unfortunately, it was not all over for Doyle, as he thought I was dating this guy who kept coming around our cafeteria table at dinner. Indeed, this guy did have designs on me, but I only had eyes for Jeremiah in the City.

After a month of pining and mad, mad flirting on my part, I had to resort to telling Doyle's best friend, Kyle, that I liked Doyle. A classic middle school move? Absolutely—that's why it's a classic. It works.

Next thing you know, it was St. Patrick's Day in Chicago, and Doyle and I were shivering in the cold on the shores of Lake Michigan's Olive Park. He had asked me out for a picnic, and after several costume changes, I ended up wearing my friend Rachel's yellow cable-knit sweater, not that he could see it under my coat. I resolved not to look like a sofa on our first date. He unpacked the bagels, cream cheese, and thermos of hot chocolate that he'd brought. He was droll, I was giggly, and both our sets of teeth clattered uncontrollably, which didn't lend itself to much conversation.

So we packed up the picnic and headed to 3rd Coast Cafe, where the bohemian warmth matched the balminess we felt inside. I had apple cinnamon tea in a diffuser, and he had a coffee drink with Torani syrup. We stopped chattering as the heat from the steaming drinks circulated everything with a warm glow. Oh, it was *on*.

If a passerby happened to glance down at the cafe in the basement of that brownstone on the corner of Dearborn and Goethe, he or she would have born witness to two college students sipping their drinks distractedly, laughing and listening, telling stories, and falling for each other. It was the birthday of their happiness. And if that person had the gift of prophecy, he or she might have seen this same duo, twenty years aged, sitting in the same cafe, this time joined by two blond-haired youths and a black-haired little girl, sharing an omelet and telling their children about the cafe's significance, remembering when their family began.

...

Much as I pined for Doyle early on, there is so much fabulous yearning in the love story of Gilbert Blythe and Anne Shirley, most of it on his part. He had no idea how unrequited this longing would be, and for how long. Over and over, as Anne swept by him disdainfully, Gilbert tried to appease her. Still, he yearned on.

It struck me anew that though Maud didn't even have the right to vote, she made the smitten boy and the stubborn girl equals and academic rivals. Anne's intelligence, though it would have been off-putting to most boys, made Gilbert like her all the more. So though Anne was pretending he was dead to her, in reality she was completely obsessed with besting him at school. Back and forth they went: "Now Gilbert was head of the spelling class; now Anne, with a toss of her long red braids, spelled him down."[9]

She spelled him *down*! And then Gil turned around and spelled *her* down too. Test by test, challenge by challenge, they were iron sharpening iron. It could have been great fun, if only Anne weren't such a ninny.

Even Diana tried to intercede on several occasions, once chiding Anne for going overboard in her grudge against Gilbert at the Debating Club recital.

I'm with Diana on this one. Really, Anne? You pretended to read a library book instead of listening to Gilbert's "Bingen on the Rhine" oration? When he came to the line, "There's *another*, not a *sister*,"[10] and looked right at her, she pretended not to notice.

Me, caterwauling to Anne through the pages: "Clearly, the hottest boy in Avonlea thinks of you in unbrotherly ways! This is Gilbert Blythe we're talking about—are you made of stone, woman? My suggestion: Shut that library book right now and gaze back into his soulful brown eyes. Mind you, don't wink at him, or he'll fall off the podium. Smile a little, give the poor guy a crumb of hope. Then, when the time is right, invite him over for some of Marilla's matchless plum puffs and a tumbler full of raspberry cordial!"

But no, Anne didn't listen to anybody when it came to "that person."[11]

If Gilbert only knew that saving Anne's life would be the catalyst that would begin to soften her heart, he would have rowed Harmon Andrews's dory in Barry's Pond every single day for the chance. But even after he rowed himself to the right place at the right time and plucked a white-faced, white-knuckled girl off the bridge piling to which she was clinging like a marine gastropod—which, *you'd think* would suffice as absolution—she didn't melt.

Instead she sat in his boat, "drabbled and furious"[12] and refused his helping hand out of the boat when he rowed her safely to shore. And instead of responding graciously to his heartfelt apology—again— and his sincere sentiment that her hair was awfully pretty, Anne chose her grudge over grace, vanity over vulnerability.

She almost lost him forever. Even Gilbert Blythe had his limits. He was angry, and rightfully so, when Anne refused to accept his apology and told him she would never be his friend. Yet something changed that day on the shores of the Lake of Shining Waters. Unbeknownst to Gilbert, Anne did feel something as she looked at the half-shy, half-eager expression in Gilbert's eyes, and it gave her mulish heart a quick, queer little beat.

It would take Anne's world cracking wide open for her to lay down her pride. A year or so later, Gilbert sacrificed comfort, convenience, and his own ambitions to give up the Avonlea school teaching position so she could remain with Marilla after Matthew's death. It was then that Anne finally saw the valiant knight before her. This makes me think about my own stubborn ways. What honor, what valiance, have I missed because of it?

This part makes me smile: When Anne extended a hand of confession and regret at long last, Gilbert grabbed on for dear life. (Literally, the text tells us Anne tried "unsuccessfully"[13] to let go of his hand.) After a five-year standoff, the good enemies had become good friends, and maybe even more, because after all that yearning, Gilbert Blythe was not letting go.

...

As Maud says at the end of *Anne of the Island*, "There is a book of Revelation in every one's life."[14] I read mine on a bitter night when I thought I might be dying. "Doyle.... Where's Doyle? ... Is Doyle okay?!" I was barely conscious and calling out for Doyle every few minutes, despite the fact that he was right by my side in the hospital, holding my hand.

Rewind four or five months, when I had been miserable. It was a slow-growing misery that began to take root when the fires of new love were tamped down after the wedding by the realities of paying the electric bill, choosing how to spend our spare time, and realizing that we were in fact—shocker—extremely different. We were going on five years of marriage, and it was the autumn of my discontent.

To no one's surprise, this coincided with hunting season, Doyle's great passion in life and my bane. We fought about the way he seemed to prefer cavorting with deer over canoodling with me. With my upbringing as a city bookseller's daughter, I couldn't begin to understand the appeal of getting up at four thirty in the morning, drizzling raccoon pee on your camo boots, and sitting in the cold and rain and snow for hours in hopes of spotting a doe or a buck. I went with him once when we were dating, clad in the petroleum camo suit his parents had gotten me for Christmas. Being from Manitoba, the cold never bothered me anyway, but it was raining that day, and to call it "morning" would have been premature. I've never been accused of being an early bird. So I fell asleep in the nook of a tree and woke up sputtering like a wet hen when rain fell in my mouth. Obviously, hunting wasn't the hobby for me.

From late August on, my husband seemed to think of nothing else, his eyes glazing over at any attempt on my part to bring up another topic. I had married Jeremiah Johnson alright, and I was stuck with him. "Oh, but you knew what you were getting yourself into," Doyle rallied when I complained about his outdoor pursuits. But the truth is, no one really knows what he or she is getting into—not really. The real decision is whether you stay when it dawns on you: *Oh, so this is what I got myself into.*

My malaise that autumn and winter went deeper than being put off by hunting. I felt alienated and misunderstood. I was a Canadian, Mennonite city girl who married into an American, Baptist rural family. (I would add to this tally "gun happy" and not offend any-one.) So five years into our marriage I wondered, *Do I belong with this family, this man, so far from home?* It surely didn't feel that way. I daydreamed about back doors and side doors and greener pastures, until the morning in January when I read my severe mercy in a hos-pital bed.

We think the brakes on Grandma Finney's car failed. I have no memory of anything, not blowing through the red light on the nexus of Burton Avenue and Madison Avenue, two seconds from where we lived; not being T-boned at forty miles per hour, not having giant metal claws exhume me from what could have been my crushed tomb. Doyle heard the crash, and somehow he knew it was me. When he saw the powder-blue Citation smashed in like a tin can, he thought

I was dead or paralyzed. He watched in helpless fear as I was lifted out of the wreckage, my head limp and blood streaming everywhere.

I didn't wake up until later at St. Mary's Hospital, and all I could think about was Doyle. *Doyle . . . I choose you! I choose you!* In my confusion, I was terrified that he had been hurt too, and it took a while before I recognized his calming voice and strong hand in mine.

The accident exposed a bone-deep truth: There would never be anyone for me but Doyle. He was the love of my life—flannel shirts, venison, and raccoon pee included. As my closed head injury and broken pelvis and tailbone healed, so did my expectations of marriage. Like Anne, I was weaned on sentimental romances in books and, unlike Anne, in movies. Our culture casts romance and excitement as our savior and rescuer—we will be healed and whole if only we find our soul mate at the top of the Empire State Building on Valentine's Day. Like Anne, I almost missed out on true love by expecting a fairy tale. (This may be why Jonathan Crombie's death hit us so hard. He had become the epitome of the soul mate we all hoped to find.)

But as I lay there in pieces, half-conscious, my terrible, wonderful book of revelation showed me this was a lie. I did belong with Doyle, with whom I had nothing and everything in common. Who were the poetry-spouting, urban-living sophisticates of my fantasies—the fish that got away—when I had a country-fried man who would turn me and my fractured pelvis over gently every time my hip cramped? They were as vaporous as the fantasies I harbored about my birth family— misty puffs of smoke and mirrors that didn't stand up to reality.

Similarly, Anne read her book of revelation that agonizing night when she thought Gilbert was dying of typhoid. As she sat vigil in her room all night long—not even able to go to Gilbert's side because they were supposedly still just friends—she realized that "she must pay for her folly as for a crime."[15] For years she had bought into the illusions of the tall, dark, handsome, and enigmatic man—a Roy Gardner or her own fictional concoction—Perceval Dalrymple.[16] Now those trickeries were swept away by the knowledge that she might never be able to tell Gilbert he was loved, so loved. Comparably, the frauds I had bought into—fantasies of bliss and soul mates and deepest belonging—were swept away by the knowledge that Doyle was my one and only.

In the words of Rachel Lynde, "while there's life there's hope,"[17] and joy came in the morning for Anne and Gilbert. Finally, she was ready to share his humble dream, of a home with a hearth fire, a cat, a dog, and the footsteps of friends. At long last, we readers receive a beautiful reckoning, a single kiss on the last page of *Anne of the Island,* the third book in the series. After almost a thousand pages of yearning, Gilbert's hopes were fulfilled, and we can only sigh with satisfaction. Anne and Gilbert's love story is meltingly romantic—'tis true—but it also reveals a practical lesson for the ages. She didn't find her happiness in diamond sunbursts and marble halls, and we won't either. Anne found hers in the boy next door, a companion with whom her brokenness was not something she needed to hide. When we find our own Gilbert, we are kept, we are seen, and we belong to each other until death do us part.

·6·

Finding Clara Macneill

This island is the bloomiest place. I just love it already,
and I'm so glad I'm going to live here. I've always heard that
Prince Edward Island was the prettiest place in the world.

ANNE SHIRLEY IN *ANNE OF GREEN GABLES*

PRINCE EDWARD ISLAND absolutely shimmers with literary ghosts, now, and twenty-four years ago—when I first set foot on the land that some call the "Garden of the Gulf" for its beauty and location on the Gulf of St. Lawrence.

My wildly anticipated first trip there took place in 1991 while I was engaged to Doyle. Since discovering Anne in grade eight, my feelings of affinity for her only grew through high school, especially when the sublime TV miniseries came out in 1986. I read the entire series as a college student, underlining especially striking bits with pink pencil.

One highlighted bit was from *Anne of the Island*:

> *"I hope no great sorrow ever will come to you, Anne," said Gilbert,*
> *who could not connect the idea of sorrow with the vivid, joyous*
> *creature beside him, unwitting that those who can soar to the highest*
> *heights can also plunge to the deepest depths, and that the natures*
> *which enjoy most keenly are those which also suffer most sharply.*[1]

Twenty-four years later, I see how my college self must have looked at those lines as if looking in a mirror.

My parents gave me a trip to PEI as a college graduation present, maybe the best graduation present ever. What could be more meaningful than presenting someone with her dream come true? It seems extravagant, but really it wasn't. At the time, airlines were handing out free flight vouchers like candy canes anytime someone was bumped off a flight. In those days, a voucher and two hundred dollars could pay for the whole shebang.

I made the trek along with my Anne-crazed friend Stephanie. We clutched hands on the ferry between Caribou, Nova Scotia, and Wood Island, PEI, and gasped when we first glimpsed the island. It was a chilly May afternoon, and the rusty cliffs and pewter-colored waves were more beautiful than we had imagined. And we were girls with great "scope for the imagination."[2]

The minute our rental car was off the ferry, we navigated our way to Cavendish, Maud's home village and the basis for Avonlea, and the Lake of Shining Waters Bed and Breakfast. The first ghost we encountered was that of Mrs. Rachel Lynde. We were told that the dear lady on whom Maud based Mrs. Rachel had lived in the very house in which we were staying. I half expected her to jump out of a closet and wag her finger at me: "You're too heedless and impulsive, child."[3] She never did materialize, but that opinionated lady seemed very near to us as we ate breakfast in her home, relishing the view of the red-dirt beach and dainty whitecaps in the distance.

Stephanie and I came to the island to find Anne, as so many other pilgrims have done, but we ended up losing ourselves in the greater story of her creator. Maud's orphan heart was stirred with the idea of another castaway, one to whom she would give everything she was denied; this resonated with me.

We walked in Maud's footsteps, tracing her path from cradle (at her birthplace in Clifton, PEI) to her ornate grave in Cavendish. Our girlish hearts thrilled as we stomped around the graveyard, seeking Herman Leard's moldering tombstone as well, knowing as we did that he had been the great passion of Maud's life. Our innkeeper told us to keep an eye out for Herman's grave, and by the time she was finished with telling us his story, we were leaning in with eyes wide open. "He was really the love of Maud's life," she said. "Not her husband, Ewan."

Herman and Maud met when she boarded as a teacher in his family farmhouse, but their relationship was to develop quickly into quite the smoldering volcano. He was *devastatingly, mind-bogglingly* handsome, and the two reportedly were smitten with each other, that is until Maud realized that Herman could not keep up with her intelligence-wise. (How she knew this I don't know because it doesn't sound like they did a great deal of talking.) Herman also reportedly told her that she was "too ambitious," which is unfortunate but was a common attitude of the day. We decided we still loved poor, hot Herman. Why, the dear gent didn't know any better! He was obviously a victim of his era!

Maud broke it off in 1898, and Herman died of pneumonia less than two years later at the age of twenty-six. She was to mourn him for the rest of her life—doesn't that just give you a little chill? Obviously, Anne would insert herself here and say with a dramatic sigh, "It's just *so* tragically romantic . . ."

Stephanie and I leaned heavily toward the theory that poor Herman had died of a broken heart. Of course he had! What other reason could there possibly be for his premature death? We would accept none of them. Meanwhile, Maud was never to find her Gilbert, or any man who supported her writing, which we found unbearably sad. Our guys championed our writing with great gusts of enthusiasm. It was hard to imagine beloved Maud writing without the essential patronage of the man who shared her life.

One evening, we pulled sweaters on and walked along Cavendish Beach in PEI National Park. We clambered up a dune and stood at the top watching the sun slip into the ocean, the sky a parfait of reds and pinks and golden tints. In that moment, we two landlocked girls understood how Anne could say that the sea was "all silver and shadow and vision of things not seen. We couldn't enjoy its loveliness any more if we had millions of dollars and ropes of diamonds."[4]

In five blissful days, Stephanie and I kept tryst with the story we loved, examining Maud's ancient typewriter at her Clifton birthplace and admiring the views she had while writing *Anne* at the beautifully kept home in Cavendish, where she grew up with her grandparents. The bookstore at the homesite is run by Maud's cousin's child, John Macneill, and his wife, Jennie, and is a feast for bibliophiles. Maud was a self-described "book drunkard" who said of books that she could not "withstand" them.[5] If she had known that there would be such a shrine to ink, pages, and story, she would have surely burst into one of her raptures.

We also strolled Lover's Lane and the Haunted Wood, and we sat reverently on the shores of the Lake of Shining Waters, a silvery pond outside of Silver Bush, Maud's cousins' home, the basis for Green Gables, and the place where Anne felt most loved.

Maybe it was its appealing hominess, but it was here at Silver Bush that missing and wondering about my birth parents, especially my birth mother, seemed to crisscross with Maud's own longing for a mother. My wedding was six months away. This fraught event revived all kinds of wistful speculating. *Could I find my first mother in time for her to come to our wedding? Would she want to come?* And then my thoughts would spin around, and I would think, *Of course she would want to come and see her firstborn child on her wedding day!*

But then again, what if she didn't?

I found myself pondering my origins more than I had in years. When I was thirteen, my parents gave me my original birth certificate, revealing my original name to be Charlene Rudineska. I obsessed about it for a while, looking up the name in the Winnipeg phone book and finding just a handful of listings under that name. I think I called a couple of those numbers and hung up frantically when anyone answered. But that fixation faded as, invariably, I became distracted by my teenaged life. Now I wondered again, *What was Ms. Rudineska thinking about me? Or was she Mrs. Somebody Else now?*

There had been clues along the way. When I had worked at my dad's bookstore during Christmas break just five months prior to my PEI trip, two things had happened there that propelled me to a deeper level of questioning and investigation. I was at the cash register one evening, and I froze when the customer handed me a dollar bill. The word *RUDINESKA* was written in black-inked, precise capital letters across the bottom of the bill. I slipped into autopilot and finished the transaction, but my mind spun like a wheel. I kept the bill and wondered what it could possibly mean. It felt like a sign, evidence in ink that this phantom family really existed in time and space.

The other clue was bigger, meatier, and also revealed itself at my dad's bookstore. And this hint actually gave me a direction in which to point my quest. I came into work one evening and there on the store counter's left side was a neat pile of flyers advertising a Christian businesswomen's luncheon downtown. The speaker was Jane Rudineska. Again I experienced a slap of shock as I stared at the name, unable to look at anything else. She was billed as a member of the legislative assembly, the equivalent of an American state senator. She would be giving an address on "Living Your Faith in the Marketplace." There would be chicken salad and chocolate éclairs. Tickets were twenty dollars per person and available at the door or by calling the number on the flyer.

It all made sense. I had always pictured my birth mother as career oriented, wearing shoulder pads and suits and coming home to a chic but lonely apartment downtown, maybe because I had always imagined myself someday as a professional woman. Could I be right? There was no picture of this woman, but I conjured up an image of crispness and capacity and a hint of warmth beneath her polished veneer. This could really be *her*.

She was political. *I* had been political since the age of seven when my brother and I were asked to pose for pictures with Prime Minister Pierre Trudeau. My mum had towed us along to the hair salon downtown where my dad's old friend from his beauty supply salesman days gave her a big discount. Trudeau and his entourage walked passed us in the hotel where the salon was located, and one of his people stopped us. Even at seven, I could tell that the PM was incredibly charming and warm. He told my mum that her children were beautiful, and his eyes twinkled as he greeted me. I wanted to grow up so I could vote for him someday, and I began avidly following his career, especially during elections.

Jane Rudineska was a member of Trudeau's Liberal party. It all had the sensation of being preordained. I felt sure that if Jane was not my birth mother, she had to be related to me. She was actually one of the very few Rudineskas in the phone book. Yet, for reasons I didn't understand at the time, I didn't attend the luncheon or contact Jane then. I wasn't ready yet, and so I shoved it to the back of my mind until the opportunity had passed. I tucked Jane's name and title away for that future day when I would be free to follow this trail.

Maud's trail to her mother was different, but she also yearned for connection and relationship. When Maud was just twenty-one months old, her mother, Clara Macneill Montgomery, died of tuberculosis, leaving Maud in the care of her father, a country merchant. As was the custom of the day, Hugh "Monty" Montgomery gave his little daughter over to Clara's parents, Maud's grandmother and grandfather Macneill.

While Green Gables itself is a faithful, polished replica of Maud's descriptions, Silver Bush inhabits the soul of the Cuthberts' home. It was here in this white and green 1872 farmhouse, while visiting her cousins and her uncle John and aunt Annie Campbell, that Maud felt as loved as she ever would in her lifetime. She could run around with her cousins, laughing and sneaking downstairs for late-night snacks in the pantry. Maud could be a child at Silver Bush. She was wanted and welcome here.

On our visit, Stephanie and I discovered that Silver Bush is a font of information about Maud and her family ties. The doors and stairs creak, and the wallpaper is wrinkled and stained in spots. An ancient, magnificent, black and silver stove sits like a throne in the entranceway, adjacent to the aged aqua-blue chest that is the focal point of the room. We are told it is the very trunk from "The Blue Chest of Rachel Ward," a story ripped from Maud's own family lore and included in Maud's best-loved book *The Story Girl.* Our guide retold the story of the bride Rachel Ward, who in her wrath of being jilted, stomped outside in her glorious wedding gown and buried her wedding cake in the front yard. Unbeknownst to her, the groom had been arrested and taken to debtor's prison.[6] Bereft, left behind, and left, Rachel was another kind of orphan.

We stared in fascination at the contents of the chest—Rachel's fairy tale gown, a dream in ivory and gold; the exquisite egg cups and linens from her hope chest, preserved now under glass. I envisioned the bride in white-hot rage, stomping, shoveling, pitching clods of earth, and dropping that poor, innocent cake in the hole as if the icing were poisonous. (I also picture the guests arrayed in their finery, being all "I know you're mad, but the cake is filled with lemon curd, after all.") She stripped off her gown, stuffed it in her blue hope chest, and demanded that no one ever, ever open it until the end of days. No one dared to do so for forty years, when Maud herself, by then a famous authoress, gingerly brought up the subject with the now aged and still single bride. "I can't believe no one has done it until now," she had said, giving Maud her permission. (Isn't that just rich? "I can't believe no one has done it until now.")

Talk about bookish spooks! We could just about hear the agitated rustle of Rachel's satin skirts brushing the floorboards amid the creaks of Maud's "wonder castle," a thought that sent tickles up our spines. Because if *she* emerged from the walls during our stay, all glimmering wraith-like, this particular ghost *would* have a shovel, and she would *not* be afraid to use it. To our credit, it was a dark and rainy night after all . . .

But Silver Bush was so inviting, so amiable that it was easy to understand why Maud had felt noticed and important and *found* here. As thoughts of my own birth mother came to me, I imagined young Maud asking her aunt Annie numerous questions about her own mother, Annie's sister, and savoring every anecdote as a gilded link to heaven.

However, it wasn't Aunt Annie who gave Maud her most cherished connection to her mother. On the walls of Silver Bush is a framed quote from Maud's journals in which she tells a sacred story:

"One day when I was in Clifton," said the old lady, "I went up to see your mother. She opened the door for me and exclaimed, 'I am so glad

*to see you. I am all alone and I just felt I couldn't endure it if somebody
didn't come.'"*

"Well, I'm here now and I'll help you out," I said. "What is your
trouble?"

"Oh," Clara said, "little Lucy Maud is so sweet and lovely to-day
and Hugh John is away and I've no one to help me enjoy her!"

*I felt as rich as a multi-millionaire when this old lady fished up out
of the deeps of her memory, so soon to be dust, this pearl for me. How
easily I might never have possessed it!*[7]

I smiled. *I've no one to help me enjoy her!* I was happy for Maud,
who gave Anne similar jewels from a lost mother in *Anne of the Island.*
I understood her longing. When you don't grow up being raised
by the woman who gave birth to you, there are wonderings and
mysteries—pieces looking for a place to fit. When Maud heard this
story about her mother, it locked into place an indispensable piece:
She had been treasured by her mother.

Some folks search all their lives to find that lost piece, their missing mother, only to be disappointed—or worse, wrecked by what
they discover. Some missing mothers are dead. Some are wrecked
themselves, which led to them choosing or being forced to relinquish
their children. Which is more disappointing—to discover you will
never get the chance to know this missing person, or to find her only
to realize she falls short of your hopes? Other birth mothers—and
most birth fathers—simply don't want to be found.

My girl and I are the lucky ones. From as long back as I could
remember, I was told by my parents that my birth mother had loved
me and made a sacrificial choice to give me up. This is the narrative
my mum and dad gave me; they believed it and passed their belief to
me like a torch.

Years later Sunny, the social worker who'd worked with Phoebe's birth mother, told me how the young woman had held Phoebe, loved her, and grieved for her. I can extend this torch for Phoebe. Maud knew, I know. Our original mothers loved us. Someday I pray Phoebe will accept this torch, carry it forward, and be warmed to the depths of her spirit by it.

...

If Aunt Annie was a link from Clara Macneill to Maud, Jane Rudineska turned out to be a major connection to my birth mother. After Doyle and I had been married for a few years, I was ready to investigate my roots. I started by tracking down Jane, who turned out to be the ex-wife of a member of my birth mother's extended family. Jane was an angel to me. She shared my faith and wanted to help, even though she had little to do with her ex-husband's relatives anymore. She told me what she knew about them and confided her belief that my birth mother was probably the oldest child, Theodora. She also offered to help me cut through some governmental red tape to locate her. A social worker from Manitoba Post-Adoption Registry traced and found my birth mother to indeed be Theodora "Dora" Smyth, née Rudineska.[8]

I immediately wrote Dora a rambling letter about my life up until that point. There wasn't a single hint of resentment in it, because that's not how I felt. I told her about my parents, the loving home I grew up in, and my Mennonite relatives, but that there had been a missing piece: her. I heard from the social worker in Manitoba that Dora had been deeply shocked by her call—and not overly friendly. Looking back now, I can understand her reaction and panic, but at the time, her guarded response fueled my paranoia that she didn't want to be found.

The weeks leading up to Dora's response were torture. I swung wildly from being sure Dora would be my new best friend to absolute dread that she would reject me:

She loves me!

She loves me not!

She loves me, probably, maybe, one would think . . .

She does not love me—probably, maybe, one would think . . .

It was like being on that hideous Sea Plane ride at Michigan's Adventure—a slow, swinging sway up to the top and then a horrific, plunging free fall toward the ground, and probably death. (Yeah, I totally cannot handle that ride. Just ask my nephews, who are now grown men. They think it's just *so funny* that their aunt Lori got on a ride with them when they were like, eight, and proceeded to squawk bloody murder, flailing and twisting, while apparently trying to climb out of the ride in midair. I've blocked this out, but just ask them. It's among their most cherished childhood memories.)

So weeks later, after flying back and forth on an emotional Sea Plane, I was enormously relieved to receive a fat letter with Dora's name in the return address. Within the first few lines, I knew I could exhale. Dora expressed her love for me, and I felt a new sense of calm and order to the world. This reunion business was going to work out my way after all.

Letters started to fly back and forth between us, each one revealing new layers of this person who had been an enigma for so long. It was like falling madly in love. Dora consumed all my thoughts and feelings for months. I learned that Dora was a writer. (When I told people this, they invariably swooned. Everybody loves a vignette that confirms the power of the blood connection.)

While I toiled away interviewing wild rock stars and delicate figure skaters on ice-show tours in my job as an entertainment writer for the *Grand Rapids Press*, Dora wrote pieces about wild mushrooms and delicate flowers found in the rain forest. While I was backstage with Def Leppard and Styx, foraging for quotes, she was in the backwoods, hunting for nuts and berries.

"So *that's* why you're a writer," people would say, nodding and beaming as though they had solved Stonehenge. I did think this writing connection was cool, but deep down I knew, even in the flush of infatuation, that this didn't quite mean Dora was the other half to my whole. I knew it was a piece of why I was a writer, but a small one. Had my latent bents not been nurtured carefully by my parents in an atmosphere drenched in words and books, writing could have so easily ended up on the "used to have a flair for it in school" landfill. My writing was sown by Dora, but it needed daily cultivation to grow. I knew my parents, especially Abe, the bookseller, had done the lion's share of advancing my writing dreams.

Nonetheless, I carefully saved each clipping Dora sent me on birds, moss, and other bewildering topics. Maybe I was looking for it, but every once in a while the beats of her stories would remind me of my own, as if my fingers had been somehow coded with her cadences.

And finally, four years later, we met in the flesh on Dora's home turf. I traveled to British Columbia by means of a tiny, shaking airplane in a thunderstorm. Poor John F. Kennedy Jr. and his beautiful wife, Carolyn, had been killed in a plane crash over water just a few months before my already anxious flight, so it didn't even take a speck of imagination to imagine my own death. No wonder I felt ill by the time I got off the plane. The moment was surreal and so laden with destiny that I may have felt a bit sick anyway. (If meeting your original mother was a sports event, it would be included in the X Games.)

Dora took me into her arms as she met me outside the Jetway. "My baby," she murmured, sniffling, hugging me close. "My baby."

I highly recommend Dora's hometown, a misty harbor village of totem poles and starfish, as a place to reunite with the woman who gave birth to you. We took long rambles in the forest while Dora snapped photos of trees, bugs, and her thirty-one-year-old baby girl. We strolled on foggy docks, scavenging for starfish and shells, and shopped for souvenirs in little shops run by coastal First Nations proprietors. There were muffins and omelets for breakfast, and salmon pulled from local waters for supper that was prepared by Dora's most excellent husband, Bill.

It was all very idyllic on one level, but uneasy on another. How was it I felt like an outsider in the home of my flesh-and-blood mother, a foreigner in supposedly native territory? Dora had bent over backward to make me feel at home, yet things felt off-center. For instance, the fact that happy hour was strictly observed at their house was so weird, but why? What could possibly be wrong with enjoying a glass of good red wine in front of a picture window overlooking the water? Nothing, and everything, when you've been raised by people who think happy hour is when *Hymn Sing* comes on the CBC on Sunday afternoons after church.

In that glorious house in its superb locale, all I could think about were my mum and dad, shoveling snow in front of a shy little green and white bungalow, with no totem poles, cruise ships, or starfish within hundreds of miles. I missed them so.

My parents had been supportive about the whole process of finding Dora and meeting her. They had been unfailingly open with as many details as they had, including my birth certificate bearing my given name and Dora's maiden name. When I look back now, I see that my mum and dad were quite a bit ahead of their time in terms of their openness toward a topic that was usually made much more hidden by the adoptive parents of their era. They were at that very moment probably either praying for us or thinking about me and

Dora. When I called them from Dora's house, I had sudden tears and no idea why.

According to Frederick Buechner, we should always pay close attention to unexpected tears, for "they are not only telling you something about the secret of who you are, but more often than not, God is speaking to you through them of the mystery of where you have come from and is summoning you to where, if your soul is to be saved, you should go to next."[9] I didn't know it then, but God was calling me back to the mystery of my roots.

I was so glad I had the chance to meet Dora—I loved her. On that same trip, I spoke to Danica, my younger half sister, for the first time on the phone. I would come to love her as well. There was no question: This family held an important piece of real estate in my landscape.

But there on an island across Canada from PEI, something new and essential began to take shape: God was speaking to me through my ambivalence and summoning me home. I was beginning to understand that my first loyalty went to my mum; my dad; my brother, Dan; and the home we had created together on Kingston Avenue. Mostly, I belonged to them. I had come to British Columbia searching for my true place on earth, only to find I had carried it with me all along.

· 7 ·

Bereft, Left Alone, and Left
(Two Birth Mothers and Daughters)

Behind all your stories is always your mother's story,
because hers is where yours begins.

MITCH ALBOM, *FOR ONE MORE DAY*

AS USUAL, MY FRIEND TROY HAD IT RIGHT. Troy is my brother, not by blood or adoption but by choice. I call him Daisy, short for "Daisy Duke," which stems from an incident a few years ago when his spectacular wife, Julie, was out of town and Troy made a very unfortunate choice of wearing short shorts at my Canada Day picnic. (I can never un-see those fish-belly white legs.)

We met fifteen years ago, picking up our babies at the church nursery. Much to my astonishment, Troy introduced himself as being from Winnipeg and within seconds notified me that he loved the Winnipeg Jets as freakishly as I did. He was adopted, too, and just ten months younger than I (although he would have you believe I am nearing dementia while he is still scampering around in unbridled youth). He was also half Mennonite, he told me, which was golden.

For starters, I didn't have to explain that I did not drive a buggy and churn my own butter. In five minutes, we understood each other perfectly. You've got to understand—most folks around these parts think Winnipeg is in some annex of Alaska. They've never heard of it, even though cultured, beautiful Winnipeg is a bigger city than Grand Rapids. And when you tell them where it is, above North Dakota and Minnesota, they carry on as if everyone "up there" lives in heated yurts and mushes their sled team through the drive-through at Kentucky Fried Beaver.

I instantly cherished Troy and Julie for understanding Winnipeg, Mennonites, and what it is to be a Jets fan, a group of certifiable lunatics who, like Winston Churchill, *never* give up hope that this is the year we will go all the way. I immediately felt as if we belonged together, our two families, them choosing us and us choosing them.

Troy is a social worker who counsels the bereaved in the context of hospice. He's wise and compassionate and very good at what he does, but one can only hope he wears appropriate pants in the workplace.

Recently, we were at a wedding reception with our spouses, and in between the chicken Kiev and Troy's ill-advised stab at line dancing, we slipped from our usual stance of giving each other the berries to solemn conversation.

Our topic was adoption and race, a thread the two of us could pick up anytime and feel as if we understood each other. My daughter is Korean; his is part Native American, a status Indian in the eyes of the Canadian government. Julie is black and white, so their three sons are also biracial. We go to a church whose congregants are all of the above plus African and Hispanic.

I asked about a friend of his, a Native American kid named Theo who was aging out of foster care. This led to talking about the great wounds of slavery in the United States and then the Canadian Residential Schools. From the 1880s until well into the 1950s, Canadian government officials and leaders from the Anglican and Catholic churches seized Native children against the wills of their parents and the children themselves, forcing them to attend boarding schools.

Being from Winnipeg, which has the largest Native American population in North America, I was familiar with the tragedy of the residential schools, where Native children, terrified and grieving, were plunged into European-American culture. The children's hair was cut to look like that of children whose forebears had come from Scotland or England or Germany. Their native tongue was banned, and their traditional names were changed from Nuttah ("My Heart") and Kitchi ("Brave") and replaced with names like Alice and Edward.

This forced name change also happened to African American slaves, Koreans under Japanese occupation, and many other people whose cultures were toppled by another culture over the centuries. It happened to my dad and aunt, whose names as children were changed from the Hebrew Abram and Sarah to Adolf and Susie when they made their terrifying trek from Stalin's USSR to Hitler's Germany. After coming to Canada in 1947, my dad's name was quickly changed back to Abram. But my *tante* Susie never changed her name back to Sarah. "Sarah suffered enough," she said.

The experience of the residential schools was cruel, especially for the younger children who were separated from their parents. I love First Nations peoples, and I have empathy for their suffering, which, according to Troy, a former social worker to the Cree and Metis, continues through the generations, embedded like bullets in their hearts.

But I also can never forget the suffering of the Mennonites, my own people, who lived through sickening loss and trauma at the hands of Stalin and Hitler, mostly Stalin. My dad's family lost everything: land, houses, livelihood, possessions, their culture; and like so many Mennonites, they lost their names. My oma lost two baby girls to starvation; one of them, Anna, was my father's twin. The blood of my two aunts, like millions of others, is on Stalin's hands.

"I've always wondered why the Mennonites suffered such damage yet mostly landed on their feet," I said to Troy. "But some of the First Nations people continue to bring those past abuses, as terrible as they are, into the present." The Anglican and Catholic churches and the government of Canada have all offered deeply felt, retroactive apologies to the Natives for the residential schools. Decades have passed, and acknowledgment of their suffering has been issued, forgiveness sought. Why wasn't that enough?

Troy, who has been through his own profound losses and injustices, remains the most positive, benevolent person I know. His compassion for others shines like the sun. I will never forget his response, said in a patient voice as kind and strong as God's. He didn't tell me I was missing a piece of the puzzle. He didn't tell me that my empathy was not enough, that I was not being politically correct. Troy just told me the truth as he had seen it: "The difference is, I think, that their children were taken away from them against their wills. When someone takes your child away from you and there's nothing you can do about it, it does something to you. Some people never get over it."

My mental picture shifted. I saw a mother seizing her daughter, screaming, weeping, and begging the stone-faced government officials not to take her baby away. If there are levels to bereavement, this mother was in the lowest circles of hell itself. And I imagined myself clasping Jonah, Ezra, and Phoebe, screaming, weeping, and begging a stone-faced government official not to take my babies away. Because I knew that was something I would never get over.

· · ·

When I think of mothers relinquishing their children, two very personal stories come to mind. One is that of my birth mother, Theodora. Here I imagine Dora's reaction to me finding her, and also how she felt when

she was pregnant with me, drawing on the original answers she gave in
the adoption paperwork and our conversations and letters over the years.

Theodora could not believe her ears. She replaced the phone in the
cradle on her kitchen table. How had she been found, exposed, after
all these years? That's what she demanded to know of the social
worker, whose gentle voice had been on the other end of the line.
Her own voice had been sharp, maybe even shrill, and she regretted
her tone already. It was just that she was so fearful. The fortified wall
she had stood watch over for twenty-seven years was falling down
around her.

Her heart thudded in her chest. *Bang, bang, bang!* She slumped
in a kitchen chair, feeble against the waves of memory that flooded
her. Bill would be home in a little while, and she had to collect herself.
The worst thing she could do right now was relive those days long
ago when she had been the most terrified and confused, the most
alone. She was afraid of utterly breaking right there in her kitchen.
But she couldn't help herself.

She had been older than many of them, in those days. She was
twenty-one and a student at a Canadian university. She had flown out
of the messy, thorny nest that was her home at the earliest possible
moment after high school, winging it to the city. Winnipeg, by very
virtue of its being three hours from her hometown, was a sanctuary.
Theodora was a sensitive creature—too sensitive, she had often been
told. It had given her a pang to leave her dear dad, not to mention her
younger siblings, one of whom was only three years old. But there
needed to be space between her and her mother. Their relationship
seemed to be charged, as if the ions surrounding the two of them
were negative. The more distance the better.

Luckily, she was smart, and she knew how to work hard. In the city, she would fend for herself, putting herself through school, supporting herself through odd jobs. She had found some friends, and with the help of roommates, she was able to pay the bills until she could graduate and really become independent. And she had her faith. The Catholic church was her comfort and haven. She went to Mass as often as she could, and at times, her heart filled up with the idea of becoming a nun.

Theodora had not counted on Tom sailing into her life one summer. Why had *this* happened with Tom and not the other boys she had trifling romances with? Tom, with his dark, flashing eyes, zesty one-liners, and wiry energy, had a kind of chemical effect on her. The ions between *them* had been decidedly positive, for a short time, anyway, like forked lightning. *Zip, zap.* Here today and gone tomorrow. Yes, she had been zapped by lighting, and now she felt slightly electrocuted, with burns unseen by the naked eye. Theodora was long past romanticizing it. She could see her younger self clearly— her vulnerability, her naiveté—and how she had succumbed out of loneliness in the big city.

Even in the rosy haze of memory, there were no wistful thoughts of sunsets at Grand Beach or strolls through the dunes or what-could-have-beens. She didn't care enough, nor was she *cared for* sufficiently to make this about romance. Theirs was not a love story. But of course, she was very drawn to him at first, and he to her.

When Theodora found out she was pregnant with Tom's child, the ground underneath her felt soft. She was sinking, and there was no one to pull her out. The thought of going back to her family in this condition was ludicrous. No, that door was shut tight.

Tom had abruptly broken up with her before she even had the chance to tell him the news. Theodora's gut told her he knew she was pregnant, though she could detect nothing other than coldness in his delivery. Tom always kept things close to the vest. But she felt that this man knew she was carrying his child and simply didn't care.

Theodora was left behind by Tom, who all but sprinted away from her and their child growing inside her. She and her baby were left in his dust. There would be no solicitous attentions from the father, no courtly offers of marriage or even money. More than ever before, she was alone.

What could she do? It was 1967. Catholic girls did not become pregnant out of wedlock. Or if they did, it was muffled like a state secret. She was a girl "in trouble," a place she had never imagined for herself.

However, Theodora considered it a bit of a saving grace that she was over eighteen and free to steer her own destiny as far as she could. There would be no parents interfering; forcing her to live in a home for unwed mothers; swearing her siblings to secrecy; spinning fictions about her working as a camp counselor, visiting an aunt in Winnipeg, attending boarding school in Saskatchewan, or having a bad case of mononucleosis. She was an adult, and as such, could take the matter somewhat into her own hands.

Yes, everyone would now assume she was promiscuous—she, a prim Catholic girl who had dreamed of the convent! Abortion was illegal, but there were backroom procedures she could avail herself of. But the thought of termination was worse than what she was going through now. Theodora was repulsed by the thought. She had no option but to forfeit this baby for adoption, but oh, how the thought tortured her.

Theodora's pregnancy was a cloaked affair as much as possible, hidden behind tent dresses and shame. She was tall and thin, and therefore she didn't show until she was at least six months along. She felt protective of her baby—"illegitimate," this little one would be called! It was as if society had spoken, and the tiny soul growing in her womb was already judged as corrupted, some kind of lawless extension of her own crimes. But Theodora knew her baby was innocent and pure; he or she deserved to live a life free of such damaging stigmas.

When she went to meet with the adoption workers, she put on a cheerful air. She combed her dark brown hair to a shine and dressed carefully. Theodora had answered their questions to the best of her ability. The questions about her were not hard: She quickly rattled off her parents' occupations and ethnicity. (Later, when she had been reunited with her baby, she discovered that the social worker had boiled down all of her ethnic information into something likely pleasing to the adoptive couple, listing "German" as her half of the baby's background.) Yes, she had a positive relationship with her family! The social worker had smiled approvingly. Her family, of course, had no idea that their eldest daughter, three hours away in the city, was pregnant and volunteering information about them to a social worker.

As for Tom, she forced herself to be upbeat. The last thing she wanted to do was to tell them what she really thought about him. What if this information damaged her baby's chances of being accepted into a decent family? "He's a wonderful person," she told the social worker smoothly and recounted what trivia she had managed to collect during their brief time together. She offered the information she had about his parents' background, though she had never met them. His last name, Gordon, seemed British to her, and so she offered that as his ethnicity. He was employed and a hard worker. Did she mention he was wonderful? Well, he was.

Theodora made one request: that her baby be placed in a Catholic home, or at the very least, a Christian home. She envisioned the flickering life inside her being baptized by a kindly priest who would gently make the sign of the cross on her baby's forehead with holy water in the name of the Father, the Son, and the Holy Ghost. She imagined a little boy in crisp whites or a small girl with a frilly white dress being confirmed in the Roman Catholic Church. She wanted her baby to have the peace and stability she had found in her own faith. That much, at least, she could hope for.

She had quit her job at a Catholic school in the summer when she found out she was pregnant. She found another job in an office, and for six months she diligently did her work each day before coming home to a shabby apartment. She kept working as long as she possibly could.

It was a Tuesday night in late March when Theodora began having labor pains. She felt panicked. What should she do? Her roommate was at work, and there was no one else to drive her to the hospital. No one had talked about what was going to happen. There was no plan, no breathing classes, not even a pamphlet about what was to happen to her body. She was unprepared especially for the grief that lay ahead and the grief that already scalded her heart. Theodora called a taxicab, figuring it was better than the city bus, and packed a few things in a bag as she waited.

Her daughter was born on a Wednesday after a grueling night of lonely labor. She had finally been taken to a room and strapped to the delivery table with harsh, white lights glaring at her disapprovingly. In the lamp over her head, she could see the reflection of her child being born. It had been as ravaging as the pain of labor to realize she had no voice over her baby's life to come.

The nurse had actually said yes when Theodora asked if she could hold her baby, just once. She stared down at the little one, all five pounds, three ounces of her.

"Wednesday's child is full of woe," she recited softly. "But not you, baby, not you. You will be so happy." Theodora was the one full of woe, not her baby. The rending was coming, and it would split her open. This she knew. But she was also undeniably filled with pride and a primal love.

"Good-bye, my baby. I love you forever." The baby's name was Charlene, although she had no doubt the adoptive parents, whoever they were, would change it. "Blessings on you, whoever you are," she whispered through her sobs. "Take good care of my baby."

She left the hospital the day her milk came in, going back home the same way she came, by herself in a cab. She was sore, exhausted, and as anguished as any mother who has had to part with her own flesh and blood. No one at the hospital offered any suggestions about how to deal with the milk that spurted out of her alarmingly or the painful engorgement that followed. When she returned to work the next day, she stuffed her bra full of Saran Wrap to keep from leaking through her starchy work blouse. Somehow, the humiliation didn't register nearly as much as the mourning. Dora was the one who had left her baby at the hospital, but nonetheless she felt as if she herself had been left behind.

Once, while sitting in her dentist's office, Dora had read in a magazine that an estimated 1.5 million women gave up their babies in the '50s, '60s, and '70s, only to return home and pretend the births had never happened. Theodora was one of them. And now here she was, twenty-seven years later, sitting in the kitchen of her home, heart pulsing like a wild thing, woozy with disbelief.

She tried to take some deep breaths. Was it really so hard to believe that her baby was looking for her? Hadn't she always secretly hoped for and yea—known—that this day would come? Wasn't that why she kept one piece of information at the bottom of every purse she had ever carried in the last twenty-seven years? If she felt the scrap of paper while digging in her purse for lipstick or gum, she would have a flash of memory and pain. Sometimes she fingered the paper like a rosary bead. It had contact information for the Manitoba Post-Adoption Registry, a place where she could register her information and thus her interest in being reunited with Charlene, whose name was not, after all, Charlene anymore. But her baby had beaten her to it.

Tom. Her heart dropped like a stone. She and Bill had moved away from Winnipeg years ago, and she'd never had contact with Tom again. Would she now have to turn the key and open that Pandora's box?

Every year, on a day in late March, she cried and missed her baby. *Was she happy? Healthy? Safe? Was her baby even alive?* She would have given her left hand for the tiniest smidgen of information! And she worried. It was possible and even probable that her baby was angry and hurt, that she would resent her for giving her away. But what choice had she had in the matter? What could she have done differently?

Over the years, the not knowing had been the hardest part. Now a door long jammed shut had been pried open. On the other side were answers to her questions. On the other side was her daughter, not a baby anymore.

...

I'm going to call Phoebe's birth mother Moon, because that is my favorite Korean name of all. I also love the name Sun, but it doesn't fit somehow; the picture I have of her is not blindingly bright and sunlit. When I think of the college-aged girl who gave birth to my daughter, she exists in a kind of lustrous light but is also somewhat obscured by darkness and secrecy. And besides, I have always preferred the moon to the sun.

I do know her last name is Kim, although that doesn't narrow it down. One in every five South Koreans is a Kim—in a population of just over fifty million. Talk about a haystack.

The rest of what I know about her is actually somewhat parallel to Dora's story: Moon was the same age, twenty-one, and living apart from her family in another city. She had a brief relationship with the birth father (I'm calling him Jin), and he proved to be a disappointment to her. Their romance ended before there was any discussion of what would happen to the baby they created together. Moon's social worker filled in some of the details—that Moon's mother had turned up on her doorstep one day and that she had been present during Phoebe's birth. She said Moon had been very emotional on the phone and when she had relinquished Phoebe.

Recently, Phoebe and I talked about her birth mother and grand-mother after seeing the moving documentary The Drop Box, about a Korean pastor's "baby box" for unwanted babies in Seoul. The film under-scored the gigantic stigma for birth mothers and how the vast majority don't go through the proper channels (i.e., a social worker and a hospital delivery), for fear of their secret coming to light.

"Your Korean mama did the right thing by taking wonderful care of you when you were in her tummy," I said. "She gave birth to you in a hospital because it was the best thing for you, even though she was prob-ably afraid of getting into trouble. She loved you very much and was so brave. And your birth grandma was also brave and very, very loving to her daughter and you. Most people in her situation would have turned their backs on their daughter, but she was there for your birth mother and for you."

Phoebe nodded stoically, processing it all. I could tell she was listening with her whole self, uncharacteristically still and somber. I felt as if I was bestowing a great gift to her heart, and I was filled with gratitude for the valor and love of Moon and her mother.

From the details I do know and what I know about Korea and giving birth to a baby out of wedlock there, I am going to imagine Moon's story playing out in a place far away from here, a place I love, a motherland I carried her child and mine away from in an orange fabric baby carrier.

Moon could not believe her ears. She ended the call on her mobile with the press of her finger. What was going on with her daughter? That's what she demanded to know of the patient voice on the other end, her social worker, the woman whom she had called for an update on her baby. Moon's own voice had been tremulous, maybe even out of control, and she regretted her tone already. It was just that she was so scared. Her baby was three months old, and adoptive parents in the United States had been matched to her. Within several months, they would travel to Korea and claim her as their own.

She slouched on her bed, overcome with thoughts and emotions. Her roommate would be home in a little while, and she had to collect herself. If she wanted to stop crying, the worst thing she could do was relive the last year, thinking of a boy who had failed her and a tiny infant of splendor and grace, wrapped like *mandu* in a hospital blanket. She was afraid of breaking right there in her bedroom. But she couldn't help herself, and the memories flashed before her as if on a filmstrip.

She was twenty-one, working at a mart in Cheonan, just ten kilometers from her home in Asan City. The train ride was short but beautiful, with bright green ginseng fields flanking the train tracks. Still, Moon had achieved some independence from her family, even if they were close by. They may as well have been a million miles away when she had found out she was pregnant with Jin's baby.

Moon had not counted on Jin. He had sailed into her life on a summer's day at the Geonbae, the name of the convenience store she worked at that spring and summer. He was the newest employee at the mart, and there had been a mild buzz of excitement among the girls when this newcomer arrived, smiling and donning the ridiculously cheery smock bearing a picture of an empty glass. *Geonbae* means "Cheers!", "Good health!", or literally "dry glass."

How had she let things go so far with Jin when all it resulted in was an insignificant relationship? Jin, with his dark, glinting eyes, dry one-liners, and crackling energy, had blown into her life like a storm. Here today and gone tomorrow. And now she was left behind, abandoned in the rubble of his casual intentions.

When Moon found out she was pregnant with Jin's child, it felt like one of those dreams when you are falling in slow motion, flailing, unstoppable, and all too real.

She could never go to her family with this news. That was an understatement. She had heard about other girls who had done the unpardonable: allowing themselves to become pregnant outside of marriage, outside of the patriarchal blood line, and they had paid for it. Some were forced by their families to get abortions, which were illegal yet rampant. Some were ostracized for life, even *if* they gave up their babies for adoption. Keeping her baby was hardly an option. Such an act would bring blistering shame upon her parents and grandparents. Moon would be branded as immoral, a failure, and a criminal, and her baby would be equally shunned. She would have a terrible time getting any kind of work, and depending on her landlord's stance, eviction was a real possibility. Moon and her baby could both end up on the streets, or as karaoke "hostesses." She shivered. Moon was caught like a mouse in a trap.

Moon would not try to find Jin. She had broken up with him before she even realized she was pregnant. Things had not turned out the way she wanted them to. He had not turned out to be the person she hoped he would be. But she was glad things had ended before she knew. What if he or his family had forced her to have an abortion because her baby was of his family's seed? She was relieved that Jin was gone, long gone.

Moon's pregnancy was concealed behind oversized hoodies and disgrace. She was tall for a Korean, five feet seven inches, and didn't begin to show noticeably until her last trimester. When she couldn't hide it any longer, she endured the biting remarks and cold stares of the customers, especially the gossipy old *ajummas* who would come into the mart with their bad perms and rubber shoes. Yes, it was a disgrace to be pregnant out of wedlock, but she was proud of her baby and treasured the feeling of the baby kicking her at night when she wanted to sleep, flipping itself over, head over heels.

One night in her seventh month of pregnancy, she answered a knock at her apartment door and was stunned to find her *eomeoni* standing there with bulging bags of groceries. Moon had managed to avoid coming home via one excuse or another, despite her mother's growing suspicions that something was wrong. Well, something *was* wrong, and now her mother could see with her own eyes what that was. Moon's mother hustled inside as if she were being followed by the police. She dropped the groceries on the floor and began to scream and wail. "*Mian haeyo! Mian haeyo!* [I'm sorry! So sorry!]" Moon cried. She dropped her head and looked at her swollen ankles. This was humiliating, but Moon knew *Eomeoni*; she would rant and rave, and then the storm would pass into calm, into action. *Aboeji* need never find out. Moon began to put the groceries away while *Eomeoni* continued to howl. She was no longer alone in this.

It was a Wednesday night in late December when Moon began having labor pains. She felt so afraid, even though *Eomeoni* had rushed to her side within the hour after her call, making who knew what excuse to *Aboeji* and her siblings. The kind social worker had talked to her during her pregnancy about what was happening to her body, what delivery would be like, but of course she wouldn't really know all the details until she went through it.

Her daughter was born on a Thursday at the very end of 2004 while a horrific tsunami swept through Indonesia, thousands of miles to the south. After Moon's own struggle and pain, there was new life, a life over which Moon had no voice at all. Even as she triumphantly pushed her out and became a mother, Moon felt a terrible sadness and dread. Yielding her tiny girl would be like a death.

The social worker had come to visit her the next day in the hospital and asked Moon if she would like to name her baby, knowing that her American parents would change it anyway. "No," she had said softly, stroking her daughter's velvety cheeks and temple. "You name her." So the social worker had named her baby *Eun Jung*, which meant "grace."

The social worker, Sunny, had been very patient with Moon throughout the process. Moon knew this. As Moon was filling out the paperwork for the adoption, she had left the "Religion" field blank. The social worker had gently prodded her.

"Are you Buddhist? Are you Confucian? Are you Christian?"

Moon had not conceded to this pressure. She refused to declare herself as a believer in anything. "Nothing," she had told the social worker, perceiving that this was the wrong answer though Sunny just nodded. "I believe in nothing." She watched as the social worker made the *Hangul* strokes for the word "none." *Eobs-eum.*

Because Moon had no beliefs in God, her response was completely true. But now she had given birth to grace, and even as she handed her baby over to the nurse for the last time, she felt a measure of favor and mercy. Where so many others had taken another road, even the path of a mother-child suicide, Moon had risked much and had given life to a daughter who would always be a part of her. And Moon would be a part of her daughter too.

It still felt like her heart was being torn from her body. It still felt like too much, too hard to bear. Hot tears spilled down her cheeks, as the nurse turned her back and walked out the door with *Eun Jung*. The social worker had tried to coach her in working through the grief that lay ahead and the grief she already felt. But could anything really prepare a mother to part with her child? Moon didn't think so— not at all.

Dispatches from the Land
of Morning Calm

Travel is fatal to prejudice, bigotry and narrow-mindedness.
MARK TWAIN, *THE INNOCENTS ABROAD*

WE RECEIVED OUR ADOPTION REFERRAL (the agency had "referred" us to a child) and photo of Phoebe on the last day of February 2005. For the next few months we waited, spring-loaded with readiness to fly to the Hermit Kingdom and meet our daughter. We and the boys talked of little else, and I made numerous Phoebe runs to my favorite secondhand consignment boutiques for little fashion-forward, girlie ensembles. We decorated her room in greens and hot pinks and bought every book we could find relating to Korea.

Finally, in June, Doyle and I received notice that we could bring home the freshly minted Baby Craker. A few weeks later, we arrived in Seoul.

Dear Everybody We Love,

After a twelve-hour flight out of Los Angeles, Doyle and I landed in hot, muggy, beautiful Korea. (And by "muggy," I mean you could steam a grain of rice under your T-shirt.) Thank God for Soo Ree Jung, a Korean lady we had met at our church back home, who was there at the airport in Incheon, bearing a bouquet of flowers for me. She drove us from the gleaming airport to downtown Seoul and the Holt Guest House. Despite my studying some phrases in a guidebook, our Korean is terrible, and having Soo Ree navigate us to where we need to be has been priceless. We collapsed in our beds upon arrival at the guest house (our room has twin beds about five yards apart), although the nightlife outside this guest house looks enticing. Outside our window is a narrow, winding alley/street with teahouses, bars, tanks full of eels, and little cafes. Apparently this area of Seoul is full of university students, which means the place is hopping long into the night.

This morning we woke up at 6 a.m. and ventured out onto the busy streets for a breakfast at the cute little Morning Tomato Cafe. The owner, "Billy," was very friendly, and he turned up the Madonna CD he was listening to in honor of us. Could he somehow sense that Doyle is a huge Madonna fan? Whatever Billy's reason, the sounds of "Borderline" have never been so comforting. Unfortunately, breakfast is not really a thing in Korea, at least not in the way we do it. I understand that rice is the usual fare. We had raw fish on the airplane for breakfast, so I was happy that I could at least order a ham sandwich at the Morning Tomato.

Billy is flat-out adorable. "On behalf of government and people, respect for you because you adopt Korean baby," he said in careful English. I think we will be sharing more Madonna mornings with him!

It is an amazing experience to be the only Caucasian people in a sea of Koreans. People are so friendly, and we get a lot of communicating done through gestures and smiles.

Tomorrow we will see our breathtaking daughter for the first time. I can hardly believe that by this time tomorrow we will have held our little one in our arms! The rest of the

plans for the day seem anticlimactic, but they are important
as well: We will attempt to navigate the Korean train system
and catch a train to Cheonan, in Ginseng country, where we
will meet the social worker who worked with our baby's birth
mother. We are very anxious to soak in as much as we can
from Phoebe's birthplace. For the rest of the week, we also plan
to visit the mountains, a traditional Korean folk village, and
maybe the DMZ (the line between North Korea and South
Korea). Tonight: downtown for some action in the bustling,
vibrant, Technicolor electric kingdom that is Seoul!

Love from both of us,
Lori

And just a day later, there she was, our longed-for girl, our bright shining star. Doyle and I had traveled halfway around the world, and God had moved heaven and earth, all for one little girl. At the Holt Adoption Agency offices, we sat and waited nervously as if we were meeting a celebrity, which we were. Phoebe was world famous to us and our boys back home. Mostly, we sat alone waiting with our hearts in our throats. This was a very different "waiting room" from the one in which Marilla Cuthbert waited for her orphan. She bustled around Green Gables, doing housework and fending off the incredulity of Rachel Lynde as Matthew stood stone-cold baffled at Bright River station, beholding the child who would change his life.

The room in which Doyle and I sat felt like a doctor's office with all the scales and whatnot, and indeed, this was where our baby and other babies had come to be examined while they waited for their new parents to come to Korea. This was our labor and delivery room, where the birth pangs of almost two years would be made manifest in our daughter. We, too, were about to meet the child who would change our lives.

And then suddenly, without any fanfare or notification of any kind, a female social worker named DJ and a woman we didn't know burst through the doors, the stranger carrying a baby in a fuzzy powder-blue romper. She smiled and handed the baby to me, turning on her heels and exiting as quickly as she had come.

We had been told we would look and smell funny to our baby, that she might be alarmed and cry. I cuddled my little one as much as I dared, speaking softly to her. I started to cry, but Phoebe remained stoic. I reined myself in because I didn't want to scare her. She didn't even seem to notice me, as she seemed fascinated by Doyle's beard. Almost immediately she reached up and stroked his furry cheeks over and over again, as he made silly faces at her.

I had forgotten how heavy babies can be when you hold them for a period of time. I felt a needle prick of sadness that I had not been able to hold Phoebe from the start of her life, that she was already so big at six months and three weeks old. And I remembered Moon's broken, beautiful loss and held her daughter and mine a little closer.

. . .

That same day we made a pilgrimage to Asan City, where Phoebe's birth mother was from, and Cheonan, where Phoebe was born. Our daughter had been returned to the care of her foster parents for the day, though we would visit her the next day and each day after that until we finally took her home for good.

The subway in Seoul was marked with English signs, a huge relief and help. In fact, the worst part was the scolding I received from a nosy *ajima,* or "auntie," on the train. She didn't approve of my wearing shorts—not one little bit. I wouldn't have had a clue what the problem was had an English speaker not been nearby to apologize and translate.

Actually, scratch the "worst part" bit. It made my day. The dear lady, in her ajima helmet perm, shook her finger at me and screeched, and it was all about wearing Bermuda shorts on a scorching hot day. I wish I had worn Daisy Dukes, just for the reaction. But let's be honest, I didn't own a pair of Daisy Dukes. That ship had sailed (and sunk). During our days in Korea, I was, at five foot five and a size 10–12, Jumbo Tourist Lady Number One. This did not make me feel sassy.

In Cheonan, we were met by Sunny. This was prearranged by me through our adoption agency. I wanted to meet with her and find out anything I could about the young woman who was Phoebe's first mother. I was thinking like a journalist—and an adoptee. Any scrap of information at all about the birth mom would give our girl that much more of a connection to her beginnings. I knew all too well what it was like to grow up knowing next to nothing about my beginnings. Thankfully, the birth mother's hometown, Asan City, was close to Cheonan, and Sunny had agreed to take us for a spin around there too. I took pictures of everything—bright green and exotic ginseng fields, buildings, shops, and people—more bread crumbs for Phoebe to mark the path back to her roots.

Sunny's English was limited, but she was extremely helpful. Sunny explained that Phoebe's birth mother had not told her parents about the pregnancy because it would bring shame to them. But one day, later in the young woman's pregnancy, her mother—Phoebe's biological grandmother—had surprised her by showing up at her door. The grandmother had been extremely upset at first, but Sunny felt it was a good sign that she had been by her daughter's side during the birth. I felt grateful that Phoebe's first mother wasn't all alone during her labor and delivery, as my own first mother had been. It heartened me to know that there had been great love between Moon and her mother. The social worker told us one more thing: The birth mother had cried "many tears" when she had to say good-bye to Grace, to *Eun Jung*. "She so sad," Sunny told us. I knew this, of course, because how could she not be sobbing as she surrendered her child? Yet to hear a firsthand account made me feel sad—and guilty.

When Phoebe was three months old, Moon had called Sunny. She was anxious about her baby and crying, wondering if she had been adopted yet, wondering if Eun Jung was already on the other side of the world from her. These things were very hard to hear, but I hoped someday they would be as pearls to my daughter. I prayed she would feel loved and wanted when she heard them.

Sunny made an appointment for us to tour the hospital where Phoebe was born, which was a surprisingly moving event. As I stood in the doorway of the very room in which our girl came into the world, I grieved and rejoiced at the same time. I mourned that I was not there to witness my child's first moments. How could I have been oblivious on the other side of the world? Yet I cheered that sacred space, where joy and sadness comingled. I considered again that Moon's bereavement was woven through my happiness like a textile, and I vowed to never forget.

There had been some levity to that loaded day: For reasons I'm still not sure of, we were escorted to the office of the hospital's chief of staff. Thankfully, we had been told by our social worker at home to wrap many little gifts for people we might meet along the way, so we were prepared with a gift bag of Michigan cherry preserves upon meeting the chief. There was a period of awkward smiling and sort-of bowing and halting little speeches—what else was new for a couple of yokels in a brave, new Asian world? The chief handed us a wrapped gift as well, and we all oohed and aahed, he over his jam and we over our humongous, plush yellow towel, embroidered with the hospital's name and address in Hangul. Best towel ever, *still*.

"My husband live in Chicago," the chief suddenly said with clear pride.

"Your . . . your . . ." I groped, sensing that "husband" wasn't what he was trying to say.

"Husband," Doyle said blankly. No help there.

"Yes, yes, my husband; he study there," the chief said, grinning proudly.

At this point, Sunny jumped in with some rapid-fire Korean.

"Oh, oh!" The chief looked chagrined and began to gesture with his hands. "My son, my son! He study in Chicago! He *very* smart!" We all agreed that this must be the case and nodded enthusiastically, repeating every word he said like parrots who'd been hit on the head. "Your son! He studies in Chicago! He is *soooo* smart!"

The meeting was concluded with some heartfelt, if stumbling, speeches about how thankful he was that we adopted a baby who was born at his hospital, and how thankful we were that he ran such an exemplary hospital for our baby to be born in.

By the way, the chief was a rocket scientist. His English compared to my Korean? Genius. I'm sure my attempts at *annyeonghaseyo* (Hello!), and *kamsahamnida* (thank you) came out sounding like "Hey-zzzooo" and "Slap-youz." Tongue and syntax can be so limited. Thankfully, despite our klutzy efforts, stomping in the land mines of language, sometimes sincerity and care can still be transmitted.

Dear Everybody,

I have quickly come to crave kimchi with every meal. It's a marvel to me that I adore a food featuring fermented ancho-vies, cabbage, radishes, and garlic, not to mention a mouth-puckering smatter of Korean chili flakes, but there you are— I need kimchi, bad!

Speaking of radishes, my baby loves 'em. On Thursday, we returned to Seoul and had lunch with the Parks, Phoebe's foster parents, and DJ, the social worker, as our translator. Her foster parents are wonderful people, and both of them appear to love Phoebe dearly. The dad is very slight, though we have seen all kinds of tall Korean men walking around. I am afraid the Team Canada jersey we brought as a present will engulf the poor man, but he seemed to love his gift anyway. His devotion to Phoebe was touching, to say the least. The loving way he and his wife said her name, Eun Jung, singsongy and musical as a wind chime, transformed it for me: Un-Jun-Ahhh with an upward inflection at the end. Her nickname is Gongju, "Princess," because, they told us through DJ, "she is most beautiful girl in Korea." We completely agree.

I'll never forget sitting on the floor of this barbecue place, across the table from my daughter and her foster mother. She held Phoebe with one arm and kept her happy by spooning pickled white radish juice from a side dish into her mouth. It reminded me of writing about picky eaters in The Wide-Eyed Wonder Years *and researching what kids eat around the world. The number one baby food flavor for Japanese babies was mashed burdock root, or something similar! Food is so culture bound, and what tastes good even to babies is so variable! This scene also gave me another pang. I missed the first six months and three weeks of my child's life; obviously her foster mom knows her a hundred times better than I do. Ping! Yet I am humbly, thankfully in their debt forever. The Parks are such humble, lovely people, and we will always keep in touch with them and send photos of their beloved Eun Jung. The foster dad touches my heart especially. Phoebe ("Peeby," they pronounced it) was obviously a daddy's girl for the first six months of her life, though the entire family, including a teenaged sister and brother, doted on her. That meal with the Parks, a family we* will always be bonded to, will be a highlight of the trip. They told DJ they felt relieved to meet us, to learn they were sending their "Gongju" to parents who were experienced and relaxed, at least compared to some of the other adoptive parents they had handed babies off to.

Back to Wednesday: With the Jungs, we roamed around the mountains and rice fields in their SUV and eventually came to the Korean Folk Village, where traditional pottery, weaving, and paintings are made by artists in the ages-old way. It was fascinating to see the ancient houses and the differences between the peasants' huts and the ornate, gabled mini-palaces of the rich. The architecture of the ancient palaces and temples is exquisite, with its ruffled tile work, the rich base colors of pink/red and jade, with swirls of pink and yellow and blue. Another highlight was swinging on these huge swings meant to be stood on, and Doyle and Yeong Jung taking turns jumping on a giant seesaw ("Neolttwigi"), propelling each other into the air.

We were told this was traditionally a women's and girl's game, thought to have begun so women in traditional Korea could see over the walls that surrounded their homes, as they were rarely allowed out of their living compounds except at night! Yikes.

We capped off the day by indulging in yet more barbecue with the Jungs, an event which yielded more humor for your reading pleasure. Upon entering a traditional restaurant, one removes one's shoes and sometimes there are slippers there for customers to wear. (Or maybe I am just inventing the loaner slipper thing to comfort myself.)

There were these slide-on shoes, like shower shoes, lined up neatly by the shoe area at the entrance, and I just assumed they were for me. It's hard to get used to walking around in socks or barefoot in restaurants! You can probably guess where this story is headed. The shoes I slid on so blithely were not on loan, *which is to say they belonged to a stranger. I sat on the floor to eat, and there was a group of men across from us, drinking Soju and eating. One strikingly handsome man kept looking at me, which I found both flattering and unsettling. Finally he waved at me, grinning, and I waved back (what else does a polite Canadian girl do?). "Shoes! Shoes!" he calls out across the restaurant. The truth of my filched footwear sank in, and my cheeks turned the color of fermented shrimp paste. He was laughing, and his ten buddies were too. I rose, wide-eyed, and began to gesture wildly, as if by flapping my hands I could communicate an apology. I must have said sorry a dozen times while meekly shuffling over to the shoe area at the front. I slipped the laughing guy's shoes off and returned to my table, continuing to apologize, while begging my Korean friends to convey my utter chagrin. Overcompensate much? Yes, yes, I do. Well, what can I say? Everyone in the place was hugely entertained, including the Jungs and my husband. I think I probably made the handsome guy's whole week.*

Overall, we are becoming more graceful, saying "Thank you" and "Glad to see you," and other short phrases in Korean. Our pronunciation has improved drastically. (For instance, I've learned that bulgogi—delicious, tender slices of beef marinated in soy sauce, sugar, sesame oil, garlic, pepper, and other ingredients—is pronounced "pulgogi," with hard g's, not soft as we thought. I was totally calling it "bulge-yo-gee," which now I see must have sounded quite hilarious to everyone who heard it.)

Goodnight from the Hermit Kingdom, where I now know to assume shoes are not on loan!

Love, Lori

We were in Korea only one short week, yet we tucked one thousand memories away, souvenirs to brush off and admire in the future. Besides the monumental moments of meeting Phoebe and her foster parents, there was a single reminiscence we talk about more than any other: the fifty-course meal with a wealthy woman named Min-Hee Pak.

We had met Min-Hee several months before our trip, when she had flown to the US to go to the opening of her brother's antique shop. She had given me her card and told me to look her up when we came to Korea to bring Phoebe home. I thought this had been merely a social nicety—after all, we met only once—but when it comes to hospitality, Koreans mean business.

Min-Hee was a professor. Her husband, from what we could gather, was some kind of shipping magnate. She was very sophisticated, as many Korean women are—crisp, aloof, and gracious all at once. After tea at the hotel, she took us to Insa-dong, a fabulous market, where vendors crowded into a meandering, endless alley. As we rummaged among the stalls selling silk, ginseng tea, jujube juice, eels, garlic, beautiful celadon pottery, hand-pressed paper, calligraphy, and everything else under the sun, I traveled hundreds of years back. Like an old piece of celadon, the market itself had a patina of antiquity and worth. For me, Insa-dong was a slice of heaven on earth. It was here we bought many of the birthday gifts—fourteen in all—to present to our daughter on her birthdays. My favorites: the sumptuous blue and inlaid ivory compact mirror and the ruby red and inlaid ivory box. Even Min-Hee nodded her imperious approval.

"I take you now to most expensive restaurant in Seoul," she said when we were done shopping, in a tone that did not invite protest. We trotted behind her obediently, sneaking smirks. Dropped into Alice's rabbit hole, we were led by foot down a warren of alleys, otherworldly with splashes of color and spicy, alien smells. Finally, we arrived at a hushed, cobblestoned courtyard lit with lanterns, where we met a man who ushered us inside.

Each table had its own private room, a serene chamber blocked out in rice-paper doors, featuring huge celadon jars, a wooden table inches from the ground, and white silk cushions on the ground for sitting. There was no menu. Soon a series of gracious female servers in pink and green and yellow *hanboks* floated in and out, bearing trays with dishes and delicacies. They bowed and bowed, and we dipped our heads in kind, unsure of what to do. There were probably twelve courses and maybe fifty dishes to try. Min-Hee urged us to try everything and by "urged," I mean "strong-armed." White porcelain bowls of kimchi and white radish and other pickled things were served and then swept away by the *hanbok* brigade. Soups of soybean and seaweed and who knows what, followed. The parade was only just beginning. Savory pancakes, porridges, noodles, and dumplings were next. We sampled and swallowed, also sipping at the Soju Korean rice wine that was poured out liberally. If there was something I knew I wouldn't like—anything with mushrooms or fermented, minnow-sized fish with unseeing eyeballs—I waited for Min-Hee to avert her eyes. This was not easy, as she seemed intent on us trying each and every item on the unending menu. If I demurred, she would give me the stink eye. Yeah, I was scared of her.

Finally, there was a dish so terrifying, even politeness or fear could not induce me to take a bite. I pride myself on being an adventurous eater. I also pride myself on remaining conscious. Doyle stepped up and took one for the team, earning maybe twenty thousand brownie points. "Eat!" Min-Hee ordered, flashing her chopsticks at us in a way that seemed vaguely menacing. "This (she stabbed her chopstick at the dish) for royal family only, in royal court!" It was, we believe, a sea creature of some kind, spiky, bony, in a gungy puddle of gelatinous soup. Doyle opened his mouth, inserted the royal mystery creature, and began to gnaw bravely. Even I could tell he was grinding through some world-class sinew. "*Mmmmm*," he moaned, his eyes watering. "*Mmmmm*." (It sounded as if he were having labor pains.)

Later, Doyle said he'd rather work in a rice paddy all day long than be King Daejon and come home to this slimy, crunchy treat. ("It was pretty much cartilage," he said later. "Slimy cartilage.") Finally, blessedly, the courses stopped coming, and it was time to rise from the silk cushions and have Min-Hee tuck us into a cab for home. We thanked her profusely because it was an incredible, generous experience we would never forget, and almost ten years later, you won't be surprised to hear we have never forgotten.

Dearests,

Today we bring our daughter home. Or, at least, we take custody of her, although custody is such a cold, contentious word. But to us, now, custody means something beautiful. It means that Phoebe will be transferred from the safekeeping and care of her foster parents and Korea to our safekeeping, care, and watch. Custody is something we have longed for. She is our daughter already, and today the journey begins in raising her as such. We love her so.

Even Billy at the Morning Tomato Cafe was sobered by the significance of this day. (By the way, you would think tomatoes abound at such a cafe, but in fact we only spotted a couple of wan red slices for my breakfast sandwich. I didn't want to offend Billy by pointing this out.) He kept Madonna at a dull roar today and very formally asked if, on our last morning, we would sign a paper on his wall with some kind of sentiment that expressed our hearts toward the Morning Tomato, himself, and the very Republic of Korea. "For example, 'I love you, Korea,'" he said gravely, handing me a pen. You know, my essay on Billy's wall would bring a tear to your eye.

I do love Korea. So does Doyle. One of the big surprises for me on this trip has been how Doyle, who is not a city slicker by any stretch, has tumbled head over heels for this thrumming, neon city, as foreign as another planet yet as familiar as a relative's home. And it is home to our relative, our daughter, and so it is home to us too. We belong here too, now.

Phoebe's foster parents and I both cried when they handed her to us. It's a mixed feeling, taking Phoebe away from her people, culture, and homeland. I know she is meant to be our child, but she will always be a daughter of this ancient and modern country. We will leave behind a part of ourselves here, and Phoebe will leave behind much more.

I love you, Korea,
Lorilee

· 9 ·

"Lawful Heart, Did Anyone Ever See Such Freckles?"

No matter what you look like, the key is to be happy with yourself.

ADELE

IN THOSE FIRST MONTHS BACK IN GRAND RAPIDS, I loved to simply watch my daughter as I rocked and sang to her. Her honeyed skin and shiny hair the color of a bird's wing took my breath away. She has the world's prettiest nose (and as a person with established nose issues, I pay attention to noses). It's like God was extra-inspired when He sculpted her nose.

The first time someone said something about *my* nose, I was about ten years old. I was having a special lunch with my best friend, Lori, at the home of our gentle, cherished teacher, Mrs. Bryskchuk (in Winnipeg, remember, every third person has a name as Ukrainian as cabbage rolls). Both Lori and I puffed up like Anne's sleeves that we, out of all our classmates, had been chosen to have lunch with our sweet teacher.

I don't remember why talk turned to noses as we sat eating egg salad sandwiches in Mrs. Bryskchuk's kitchen.

"Your nose is cute and pudgy," Mrs. Bryskchuk said to me mildly, smearing mayo on her sandwich.

That's what she said. What I *heard* was that my nose was ugly, fat, too big, too prominent, too much of everything.

I laid down my sandwich, deflated, and fought the tears prickling my eyes. I did not react as Anne did, with rage and indignation. I just got really quiet and pink in the face. My beloved teacher had just confirmed my worst fears about my nose, my face, and my looks. They were not enough, in combination, to be beautiful. My nose ruined my face. My face was not enough. *I* was not enough.

Those old nettles that sting and smart and hurt more than they "should" (an abominable word) have a way of enduring. My friend Celine was insulted one day on the bus and admits to never really recovering. "I still wear glasses at nearly fifty years of age because of a day in high school on the bus," she said. "I was excitedly wearing my new contacts, and Alan P. said I looked like a horse."

(A horse? Alan P.: Have some couth. And also? You're a horse, too, and a chucklehead.)

Mrs. Bryskchuk had meant no harm. How could she have known that my nose, like Anne's red hair, was my raw nerve?

. . .

Speaking of old nettles, Mrs. Rachel Lynde comes to mind. She came on like a blunt force instrument on any topic of discussion but was especially forthright about Anne's appearance. Why, the first time they met, Mrs. Rachel found Anne's raw nerve immediately.

"Well, they didn't pick you for your looks, that's sure and certain,"[1] she said, by way of saying "hello."

Mrs. Rachel continued her laundry list of Anne's shortcomings:

Scrawny.

Ugly.

Blitzed and bombarded with freckles. Lawful heart!

But it was the last slur that shoved Anne right off the edge: Her hair, the Old Nettle opined, was the exact same tinge as a certain root vegetable that shall not be named. Mrs. Rachel named it anyway.[2] (Here, Gilbert Blythe might have taken notes.)

At this point in the book, if it wasn't bad enough that Anne was still an orphan on trial for a permanent home, wearing a short, tight, scratchy dress that accentuated her spindly legs, now the town pot stirrer was heaping abuse upon her gingery head.

Sensitivity about one's looks is a theme in *Anne of Green Gables*, one that has surprisingly savvy applications for our beauty-obsessed society. Today we might call it a conversation about body image, air-brushing, real women, etc. The truth is, we all have our sore spots, and we can lean in and seek truth from Anne and how she handled her own beauty issues.

What happens next in the story, after Mrs. Rachel bludgeoned Anne, is a boon to the heart of anyone who has ever been called scrawny, fat, homely, mousy, freckled, pale, flat-chested, chinless, chin-full, frizzy-haired, flat-haired, mustachioed, bat-winged, or pigeon-toed. (Anne would give me proxy to dedicate what happens next to anyone who has ever been called *anything* unkind.)

Anne pushed back. She had an atomic reaction, the likes of which Mrs. Rachel had never before seen. Anne sprang into Mrs. Rachel's face, quivering, trembling, and raspberry-red with rage. "Passionate indignation"[3] blew out from Anne like gasses and vapors.

Anne used the word *hate* four times; Maud used the word *stamping* in equal measure to describe Anne's feet.

Our girl lobbed a few grenades of her own, notifying Mrs. Rachel that she, too, was ugly, adding, in so many words, that she was also as big as a silo and about that interesting.

Stamping, stomping, bursting, and slamming, Anne was finally carried away on a funnel cloud of wrath, leaving Mrs. Rachel and Marilla with mouths ajar.

"Well, I don't envy you your job bringing *that* up, Marilla,"[4] declared Mrs. Rachel, not even able to refer to Anne as a human being.

Of course, Mrs. Rachel might have considered her own lack of humanity here. I mean, really! She met a vulnerable child whose upbringing at that point would have been unsuitable for a mangy dog and then wounded that child further? That is not okay—for the Victorian era or our own.

No wonder Anne had a conniption.

I know, I *know*. Anne was eleven and out of line. Had I been Anne's mother, I would have talked to her about appropriate anger management and honoring our elders. But this talk would have come long after the drying of tears, many cuddles, and at least one trip to the neighborhood ice cream place for blue moon ice cream in a violent shade of turquoise that does not occur in nature.

I've heard that it takes thirteen positive, uplifting things said about you to remove the bite of just one injuring word. (I have no idea if this is true, but whenever I've made my kids produce thirteen compliments for their maligned sibling, it works wonders.)

So if Anne were my girl and she was called scrawny and ugly, and if her hair color was blighted by a battle-ax, the situation's repair would call for thirty-nine sweet praises. I would tell her that Mrs. Rachel's bruising words indicate something black and blue inside of Mrs. Rachel, otherwise she never would have said such hurtful things.

(I would go a little teeny bit Mama Grizzly on Mrs. Rachel Lynde, too. I'm not talking about a mauling, per se, but maybe a few roars and an air swat of the paw. *You hurt my young, you deal with me.*)

So far I've been lucky. No one has said mean things to Phoebe about her face—to her face, or mine. I mean, she's beautiful. Just look at her! Okay, I'm biased. So sue me.

But: There is a certain kind of prettiness prized in our American culture, and Phoebe doesn't have it. Her hair is too black, and her eyes are too sloped. We don't live in Korea, but we do live in Dutch/ Polish Grand Rapids, where you can't throw a stone without hitting a blonde, blue-eyed somebody.

Moms worry, am I right? I worry that someday Phoebe will feel like her looks aren't enough, that she's not enough. I worry that teenage boys (not the most nuanced demographic) might overlook her foreign loveliness for the familiar and commonplace. I also worry about the opposite, that she will be objectified as an "Asian exotic," diminished in men's minds as some kind of submissive geisha. She's far prettier than I am, yet my girl will have a different and more challenging experience navigating the waters of beauty and identity.

I don't know what it feels like being an Asian in a white world, but I do know what it's like to feel like my looks fall far short of the ideal.

We all have tender places, our red hair and pudgy noses and minority colors and marginal facial shapes. No one escapes, not even our friends the supermodels! They often report feeling gawky and gangly during adolescence. (I interviewed a model once, and she told me—bless her gaunt heart—that she sometimes just wished she could eat an apple before a photo shoot. I hung up the phone and ate an apple in her honor.)

Anne's struggle with feeling unbeautiful is a recurring motif of her story, one of her most relatable points. Her particular quest to accept her red hair—her "lifelong sorrow"[5]—is pitted with obstacles. She dreams of hair "of midnight darkness" and skin with "a clear ivory pallor."[6] (This sounds like a vampire to me.) She looks into her bosom friend Diana Barry's face and sees that for which she yearns: "lovely dimples, like little dents in cream."[7] (What a coincidence. I have little dents in cream . . . on my thighs.)

So let's go back to our tableau in Avonlea and watch to see not only how Anne dealt with Mrs. Rachel's insults, but how Marilla, the greenest of mothers, dealt with her red-in-the-face girl.

First, let me say, I would have handled the situation with Mrs. Rachel differently than Marilla did. Most of us would have. She gets some slack for being a surprise recruit mom at this point. Anne's only been at Green Gables for two weeks. But Marilla *was* a mother, whether she knew it yet or not. The stoic old maid was finding parenthood's learning curve to be steep, but she wasn't as lost as she thought she was. There in the rubble between her oldest friend and this peculiar little girl who just might be allowed to stay in her home, Marilla opened her mouth to say she knew not what.

. . .

When Marilla spoke, all moms new and vintage should have listened in. What she said is nothing short of an exposé of her heart. She pushed back, advocating for Anne in a way that surprises us all—and her most of all.

"You shouldn't have twitted her about her looks, Rachel,"[8] she said flatly, later adding that Mrs. Rachel had been too hard on Anne.

You were wrong, not Anne—the girl I'm becoming so fond of, though I can't believe it. She was wrong, too, but you hurt her, and that's not acceptable.

Mrs. Rachel did not take this well. Like all bullies, she was thin-skinned and flooded with pique that she should be found in the wrong.

"Well, I see that I'll have to be very careful what I say after this,

Marilla, since the fine feelings of orphans, brought from goodness knows where, have to be considered before anything else."[9]

Now you're catching on, lady.

Though Mrs. Rachel responded defensively, just maybe Marilla's rebuke hit a teachable spot deep down. Maybe it's because we know how Anne's and Mrs. Rachel's relationship blossomed later on in the story, but something makes me believe that Avonlea's Queen Bee knew she had crossed a line and regretted it.

Rachel Lynde meant to swipe at orphans in general with her "fine feelings" comment, which reveals again her prejudice. But I thought it was an interesting remark, all the same.

Just because an orphan may not have found her place of belonging doesn't mean her fine feelings don't have to be considered. In fact, her feelings may be finer than those who have always belonged.

...

When I first was reunited with Dora, she laughed when I told her about my nose qualms, not in ridicule but in solidarity.

"I have the same nose, but now I like it. It fits my face."

It fits my face. Those four words of healing went a long way to reconciling me and my nose. It was one of those moments that seems small but was anything but.

No longer an insecure child at the mercy of a harmless comment, I had long since retired teenage fantasies about nose jobs. Somewhere at the end of high school, I even stopped shading it with brown eye shadow to "contour" it as *Seventeen* magazine suggested. I was beginning to change my expectations to fit my looks, rather than changing my looks to fit my expectations. I realized—slowly—that a teeny, wee button of a nose on this countenance would look ludicrous, after all. My nose did not ruin my face; it belonged there!

To accept one's raw nerve is all well and good, but when someone "twits" us about it? That sore spot never quite goes away.

Several years ago, when I was in the midst of writing a memoir with Lynne Spears, Britney Spears's mother, someone twitted me. Cobbling together child care, dealing with nonstop phone calls and e-mails, and rushing hither and yon as I tried to write this much-hyped tome was taking its toll. I was exhausted, physically and emotionally.

Whereupon I found myself ambushed one day during a quick errand by a man whose filter was even hole-ier than Alan P.'s. He was an acquaintance whom I ran into one day in the parking lot of the bank. I was politely trying to extricate myself from a prolonged conversation when the bomb dropped.

"Has anyone ever asked you if you were Jewish?" he asked me quizzically, as if he was dying to know.

I honestly thought he was going in a completely different direction.

"Oh, you mean because of Jonah's and Ezra's names?" I replied, innocent as a lamb. We had chosen Hebrew names from the Bible, and Ezra especially was ahead of the popularity curve.

"No," he said, shaking his head. He made a loose cupping motion with his hands, one hand up at his head and the other one just below on his face.

"Because of your *nose*. And your *forehead*."

I swear to you, he italicized.

He used quick, billowing motions, extending his hand back and forth from his nose, somewhat like the double "trombone" gesture in charades, made to indicate that one could no longer see things close up.

Blood rushed to what felt like my whole upper body. My knees felt weak, and I placed a hand on the hood of my minivan for support.

"My . . . what?" I couldn't develop a sentence to save my life.

"Your *nose*," he said more deliberately, as if I were a bit slow. He

continued with the dramatic gesticulations. "And your forehead."
The trombones played on. It was like a mime performance for one,
right there in the parking lot.

As I reeled, the stunning bigotry in his comment wasn't uppermost on my mind, but even then I realized he had crossed all kinds
of lines.

"I . . . Oh, well." I was paralyzed into vacancy. I wobbled to the
car and drove off like a bat from a dark place. Once out of this man's
vision, I erupted into tears.

My emotional response surprised me. What did I care what this
person thought about my nose? After all, it wasn't as if Colin Firth
had just insulted my facial features. The filtration system between his
brain and his mouth worked like using a laundry basket as a bucket.
Pretty much everything just spilled out.

I was thirty-seven years old, a socialized adult who knew that in
these cases one must consider the source.

However, I felt as if I'd been slugged in the stomach. How dare he?
I patted my embattled cartilage. *I still love you, nose, old friend! Well,
perhaps "love" is too strong a word. But accept you, yes!*

I was suddenly beset with concerns about my forehead. Certainly,
it was not a Cindy Crawford number. I've worn bangs all my life
because I just look more attractive with them. My forehead wasn't my
favorite feature, but I hadn't been aware up until then that it merited
dramatically mushrooming hand gestures.

Thankfully, by the time I got home, I had reined myself in. My
forehead was just fine, thank you, and if not, my bangs covered it
anyway! And my nose? By jingle—it still went with my face, no matter what this crass cat had said.

Soon enough, my outrage shifted, from my stinging ego to the
astounding anti-Semitism in his words. I thought of my beautiful

Jewish friends and their beautiful noses, and I feared for humanity anew.

...

Back in Avonlea, Marilla was plunged into motherhood's deep end, confronted with a fine kettle of fish and Anne's heartbreak. It's a masterstroke of Maud's writing to have empathy-challenged Marilla recall a long-ago hurt: "What a pity she is such a dark, homely little thing,"[10] Marilla had overheard one aunt of hers say to another when she was a child.

In that moment, Marilla softened, as we all should when empathy clarifies our understanding and relaxes our stubborn hearts. Empathy reminded Marilla that she knew what it was to be stung as is by a wasp with careless words. She understood as Anne could not that waspish words could loiter for years and shape one's sense of worth and beauty.

Marilla's maternal instincts awakened. She understood, too, that we develop sturdier hides when we grow older, but that aging itself brings a new set of concerns, far from the consciousness of The Young and the Pore-less.

I recall the time a relative told me cheerfully I had put on some weight, in skewered, congratulatory tones.

"Living the good life, I see," she laughed heartily. I did not shove her face into the potato salad.

Or there was the time when someone whose opinion mattered much to me crooned sweetly, "What chubby cheeks you have, my dear." I felt like Hansel, about to be stuffed into the wicked witch's oven. This same person took to calling me "Dumpling" for a time, until I insisted to her great surprise that she stop it and find a less shaming nickname for me. "Like 'Cheese Straw,'" I suggested. It didn't stick.

Don't get me started on cellulite.

Or wrinkles.

Or stinking liver spots, for the love of all! It's a dark day dawning when one notices a brown blotch the shape of Madagascar on one's face, and it's bigger than any freckle has the decency to be.

My chin has fallen, and it can't get up. Other parts have tumbled as well.

I may or may not have this aberrant eyebrow thing that sticks out of my face like a small antenna. Thankfully, it's noticeable only in a certain light. Yes, aging brings with it plenty of opportunities to be sensitive, but luckily, by and by, we get over ourselves more quickly than when we were young and frolicsome and merely freckled.

Once when she was bubbling over with happiness, Anne told Marilla, "Just at present I have a soul above red hair."[11] Good thing I usually have a soul above my nose (and forehead, cheeks, and thighs).

By the time we hit a certain age, we can also hope that most people are going to be a little kinder and gentler overall. I hope that about myself most of all.

In this world we will always have with us (and in us) the poor in diplomacy. We will always have people like sweet Mrs. Bryskchuk who don't even know how much their words cost us. We will always have with us the Alan Ps and the Mrs. Rachels, who step on our private land mines and trip our hidden wires. The question is, what are we going to do about it? How are we going to handle our beauty issues, and those of our daughters?

...

On the short road between Green Gables and Mrs. Rachel's, we as readers learn more from Anne on how to cope when someone vexes our vain spots. I watch with glee as Anne walked down the road, buzzing with an idea that would elevate her coming apology from an act of contrition to a piece of theater.

She had already stated her preference for life in a dungeon that crawled with snakes over making an apology to Mrs. Rachel, but her stubbornness had been unexpectedly swayed by love. Against punitive measures she would not budge, but the tenderness of a father figure could move mountains.

Dear Matthew, already smitten, put in his oar, despite his promises to the contrary, and suggested Anne smooth things over with Mrs. Rachel. When Anne believed she was apologizing for Matthew's sake, everything changed. Their relationship was already beginning to transform her.

Once at the Lynde house, the curtain opens: Anne flung herself body and soul at the very mercy seat of Mrs. Rachel.

She inserted a tremor into her voice.

She laid it on, thick and sweet as molasses, listing all the ways in which she had transgressed Mrs. Rachel and throwing in a few more for good measure. I suspect she had even convinced herself that she should apologize.

She begged for forgiveness.

And then, just when Mrs. Rachel was squirming like a bug under glass, Anne played the orphan card: "If you refuse it will be a lifelong sorrow to me. You wouldn't like to inflict a lifelong sorrow on a poor little orphan girl, would you, even if she had a dreadful temper? Oh, I am sure you wouldn't."[12]

I am also sure she wouldn't. And she didn't.

Talk about heaping hot coals on someone's head. I bet you Mrs. Rachel's ears had smoke curling out of them for days.

The two foes became friends before the sun set on the Lake of Shining Waters that day. Anne had won her over.

In Scripture, the apostle Paul talks about winning people over—the neighbor, the husband who doesn't believe, the weak, the lawless. When we are insulted and defensive, how can we turn things upside down as Anne did? How can we, swayed by love, win our foes over?

Mrs. Rachel acted abominably, but Anne also behaved badly. Yet in this messy situation, grace, love, and creative apology were the victors. See how everyone was changed by the encounter? Marilla sipped her first taste of that shielding, fierce fury, the kind only mothers have, and advocated for her child. Matthew, swayed by love, took a risk for Anne.

Anne was not quite changed enough to avoid dying her hair green a few months later, but in this particular episode she came out ahead. She pushed back, and that was the right thing to do. She stood up for her humanity, and after a time of—let's call it *reflection*—she used humor and theater to win over Mrs. Rachel.

I wish I would have had Anne's vigor that day in the parking lot, the wherewithal to stand up to Laundry Basket Face and tell him it was not okay to say those things to me, or to the Jewish race. Because it's beautiful to stand up to bullies and oppressors.

I want to teach my daughter how to act when someone trips her wires and that it's okay to be angry but not to sin. I want to teach her the difference as I continue to understand it.

I hope she discovers the beauty in her otherness, in amber skin, inky hair, and eyes the shape of watermelon seeds. May she also look for and praise beauty in others, and develop irresistible inner loveliness that draws and warms people.

10

I Love My Adopted Child Biologically

*Anyone who ever wondered how much they could love a child
who did not spring from their own loins, know this: it is the same.
The feeling of love is so profound, it's incredible and surprising.*

NIA VARDALOS, *INSTANT MOM*

QUESTIONS I GET ABOUT MY KOREAN DAUGHTER:

"Do you know anything about her *real* mom?"

"Do you think she'll ever find her *real* mom?"

"Are you her *real* mom?"

(People often italicize this word in case I am a bit slow on the uptake and don't catch their meaning.)

And once, at the grocery store, from the cashier: "Are you her nanny?"

Snarky answers:

"Yes, in fact, I know everything about her!"

"She should have no trouble because they live in the same house."

"Yes! Her hologram mom is much less attractive."

And to the woman at the checkout, "She couldn't afford me."

I know, I know. I should be nicer about the whole thing, and mostly, I am. I understand that by "real," folks are trying to say "biological" or "birth." They don't have the right words to wrap around a complex relationship. Still, it hits me sideways every single time.

My girl has used this line with me, and it doesn't just hit me sideways. It hits me like an arrow to the heart. *Bull's-eye.* "Will I meet my real mom when we go to Korea someday?" she asked me once, out of the blue. I knew what she was asking. I knew she, at eight, nine, or ten, didn't have the correct language, either. But oh how it hits that bull's-eye, every time.

I know Phoebe doesn't mean to hurt me. I said the same sort of thing to my mum years ago.

Where does this come from, this use of the word *real* to describe biology and genomic links?

I would like to call for a halt to this word in this context. Because like *orphan*, I do not think *real* means what you think it means.

Real: actual, physical, material, factual, tangible, existent, genuine, authentic, valid, true.

It describes the ways moms are with and for and there for their children, 24/7, actually, tangibly, and genuinely, does it not?

The antonyms of *real* are even worse:

Nonexistent.

False.

Fake.

Artificial.

And don't get me started on *natural.* ("Do you think Phoebe will ever want to search for her natural mother?" *Gahhhhhhh!*)

"*Natural* makes me think of organic, gluten-free, dairy-free," said my friend Sheri, who adopted the African mini queen Nkia after being her foster mom. Nkia, with her majestic long braids and strong, tall body, found a place of belonging in a household full of big brothers and a mom and dad who thought their family was complete until this little three-year-old girl needed them. Much like Marilla and Matthew, they needed her even more.

Nkia is Sierra Leonian by birth and Dutch/Puerto Rican via

her forever family. She's even a little Haitian through her brother Shelton, adopted from Haiti a few years before Nkia came along. The way Nkia fits in with her family is as organic, whole, and pure as plantains (for *tostones*) or kale (for Dutch *boerenkool*) planted in a community garden.

I know an adoptive mom who makes her own vegetable dye for use in cake decorating. In the food she's feeding her family, this mom can check off everything as organic, gluten-free, dairy-free—not to mention grass-fed and rBGH free. She may also be a sprinkler of flax seed and whey. She's a natural wonder, a wonderful mother, but apparently, according to many people who perpetrate the word *natural* in this circumstance, is mothering her children on some sort of "unnatural" pretense.

Yeah, that word's gotta go too.

Or at least, we should be using those words to describe both biological and adoptive mothers, especially the word *real*.

Dora is a real part of my story, as is Moon in Phoebe's story. So per "real," let me give credit where it's due. To birth mothers, including mine and my girl's, who step up in an extraordinarily real way for their children, thank you. Most of you made a brave choice to surrender your child to another to be raised and loved.

Whether or not you ever have a relationship with your child, your journey together continues through the years, through love, prayer, thoughts, and yes, DNA. Speaking for adoptive moms everywhere, we think of you always and tell our children you love them and did the best you could.

You are real moms.

And to moms who have been told over and over again, in ways subtle and blunt, that your role in your child's life is somehow a fraud, as artificial as Popsicles with red dye, you know better.

You are the actual mommy who soothes her crying baby, banishes monsters from under the bed, and calms her fears in a thunderstorm. You are the factual mom who sits in frozen arenas and on the sidelines of soggy soccer fields, cheering until your voice goes croaky. You are the authentic, valid, and true mom who takes the call from the principal, the friend's mom, maybe even the police.

Spirals of DNA are responsible for characteristics such as brown eyes, but a parent's devotion shapes traits of character. Features such as love, joy, and peace, patience, kindness, and goodness, faithfulness, gentleness, self-control . . . against such there is no law.[1]

We love our adopted children biologically, regardless of the fact that we didn't carry them in our wombs or deliver them. Follow me on this: If people equate "real" and "natural" with biology and physiological makeup, there is a verifiable chemical component to bonding. It's not DNA, but it is chemistry.

When we hold our children close to us, our brains and theirs release opiates, which is why we both feel physically better after a good snuggle. Holding Phoebe on my lap after a hard day at school, rocking her back and forth, and crooning words of support and care, actually doses her with a pain-numbing anodyne that soothes and settles her. It restores her peace in spirit and body. Another "feel better" compound released by loving touch is oxytocin, which scientists call the "cuddle chemical."

Any kind of love, including a mother's, dwells in the limbic brain. Through touch and talk and care, we're able to form, in ways perhaps more profound than we've imagined, the orb between our child's ears.

Each time my mum rocked me, squeezed me in a hug, rubbed my back—all this is bundled in my limbic brain's memory. Phoebe would fight her naps as a baby and toddler, and I would draw gentle little circles with my finger on her cheek or temple until she finally sank into sleep—another kind of limbic love note. Over the course of thousands of cuddles, hand holds, and forehead kisses, the neural notes become imprinted and shaped, much the same way PEI sea glass is sculpted by the eddies of the sea.

A mother's love changes the chemicals and structure of her child's brain for the good; so does the love of a father. Love is biology— a continuous life-giving and shaping force throughout the years. Clara adored her baby Maud, just as Dora and Moon loved the girls they had to surrender. Their love notes remain tucked away deep in our minds.

When I was swiped from that hospital at two weeks of age, my forever mum took up her pen and wrote countless notes, building on the ones left by Dora. I am adding to Moon's collection every day I get to be Phoebe's mother. All the hard things in this world cannot overwrite a mother's love, whether she gets to be a birth mom or an adoptive one.

So for those who are concerned about a biological connection, look no further than the next time you touch your child. Look no further than love.

Dora gave me life, and my mum shaped it. Moon gave Phoebe life, and I am forming it. One mother was a guiding star; another the North Star. Nothing could be more natural. Nothing could be more real.

11

Reunion Vignettes

Alles gut.

GRANDMA LOEWEN

THIS IS HOW THE SCRIPT READS:

You are adopted at birth by a childless couple, and you grow up happily enough in that family. But of course you aren't ever totally understood. You don't look like them, and this pains you. They all have blonde hair and blue eyes and short torsos, and you have brown hair and brown eyes and a long torso. You have a talent for drawing that no one else in your family has. Where did it come from? Then one day, when you grow up, you see a television program about birth mothers looking for their birth children. You look up in surprise when you hear a woman with a familiar voice say that she gave birth on your birthdate. She has brown hair and brown eyes and your same cowlick. It's her! You dial up the talk show and give them some of your personal details, which match the guest's exactly! You are flown to a land far, far away where you lay eyes on your birth mother on national television. You are astonished (but not really) that she is wearing the exact same sweater as you! The audience *oohs* and *aahs*, and the talk show host wipes away tears. A magic wand is waved, and you are now perfectly whole and complete, lacking in nothing. Your birth mother completes you. The reunion completes you completely. And the two of you shall live happily ever after, finishing each other's sentences and buying each other sweaters.

It's the basic draft for how people want your reunion story to go. They eat this junk up, latching on to any little detail that would make *their* version of *your* story come true. For example, when I mention that Dora is a writer, too, people get weak in the knees. Never mind that she's a nature writer. (She can be found lying down in bogs, waiting to capture elusive flora and fauna on film. I, on the other hand, have never willingly lain down in a bog.)

Society craves the fairy tale. They hanker for the cowlicks and the sweaters and especially the perfect reunion. On a related note, I read a statistic once that said up to 60 percent of folks polled wished they were adopted. My theory? People want a back door, an escape hatch from their own flawed families. They believe that if they *were* adopted, they would get a second chance at a family, one with whom their current problems and dysfunctions would vanish. Then they would live happily ever after, fade to black.

I'm here to tell you that this fairy tale is fractured. Reunions almost never work out this perfectly, and often they create almost as much upheaval as they do closure. It's not all bad; in fact, some wonderful things often come out of connecting those dots. But it's a total can of worms, and they don't call it a can of worms for nothing, eh?

July 2006

As if it wasn't enough to fly alone with my three young children to Winnipeg to visit my dying dad, I decided it seemed like a good idea to spend a night with my birth mother and her family at a cottage on Lake Winnipeg.

Dora was turning sixty and had planned this overnight visit as a special time of bonding and reunion with her daughter, my birth sister, Danica; her grandson (my nephew); and other assorted bio relatives. They would make the drive from Calgary to coincide with our trip to Winnipeg, and we would all spend time together at the cottage.

Below the surface, I was a mess. My father had been diagnosed with stage 4 lung cancer eight months before, and his life was ebbing away. We just didn't know when. It horrified and wounded me to see my chubby, jovial dad so grey, scarecrow thin, and as weak as a bird. Every day spent with him was precious. Our visit was all too brief, and I felt incredibly guilty leaving my parents at their apartment, at once frantic to get away from the inevitability of death and yet desperate not to leave my dad's side. But Dora had made a huge effort to put this together. It was important to her. I wanted to please her; I didn't want to let her down. And my parents were gracious about it. They must have felt strange, bidding their daughter and their grandchildren good-bye as they drove off to form ties with the woman who had relinquished them all thirty-eight years before.

Maybe it was painful and a relief, both. With us gone—even on such an errand—my mum and dad could go back to the shelter of each other without having to pretend things were just swell. I didn't know that these days were our last with my father. I didn't know he would be dead within a week. Yes, I would have done things differently if I had known that.

My nerves were frayed long before I'd finished the 100-kilometer drive to the cottage. Twenty-month-old P hated her car seat, the drive, the sun in her eyes. She screamed and whined, writhed and bucked and kicked my seat. At one point, she thrashed so strenu-ously she actually got herself loose from the car seat and had plopped herself on the floor of the car. I pulled over on the highway, cars and trucks thundering past me, and wrestled her back into her seat, my insides boiling.

With each mile, I geared myself up for what was to come. I would be spending time with Dora and her husband and daughter, as a fam-ily unit. My children would meet their biological cousin, Danica's nine-year-old, for the first time. Dora would meet Phoebe for the first time. How would she treat her?

We would be meeting Aunt Liz, Dora's sister, a folk dancer who alternately went by the name Lotus. All of us would spend the night together at the cottage like one big happy family.

Dora was waiting on the porch of the cottage. She came out to the car as soon as I had switched off the ignition. "Hello, my darlings!" Dora said effusively as we emerged from the vehicle, the boys smil-ing shyly at the stranger who was their grandmother. I tried to look serene while extrapolating a screeching baby from her instrument of torture.

Thankfully, the change of scenery and the new faces calmed Phoebe down. She was fascinated by Aunt Liz's dog and Aunt Liz herself, who was good with kids and blew bubbles with Phoebe on the porch for a good chunk of the afternoon. At that point, I must say, had Aunt Liz suggested she raise Phoebe herself in a tribe of Nordic Polska dancers, I might have handed her over.

Spending a couple of days at the lake was both diverting and unsettling. I had forgotten how beautiful Manitoba beaches were, the sand like powdered sugar. Lake Winnipeg reminded me of Lake Michigan—vast and moody, with no end in sight. The surroundings soothed my frayed nerves, and the earthy smells of lake water and pine trees drifted around me, encouraging me simply to *breathe in, breathe out.*

Yet this reunion business was bewildering at best. Even as I welcomed the warm embrace of the sun and the comforting sound of the waves, I knew my dad was still dying. The unknown was so terribly unsettling. I've since come to realize that it's sometimes worse to agonize and wonder how a loved one will die than to learn of the actual death itself. All the time we were at the cottage, my conflicting loyalties were pinging inside me like a black box at the bottom of the ocean.

But there was something right, too, about being on that beach. We enjoyed hanging out with Aunt Liz, who was rocking a black bikini. Aunt Liz's personality was chummy, languid, and loose in the joints. She jangled with bracelets and good vibrations. (Note to self: Folk dancing is obviously good for the stomach, if one's aunt has a better stomach than her non-folk-dancing niece.)

It felt natural to listen to my biological sister, Danica, tell me about her job and friendships. I had met Danica for the first time several years before, when Dora flew her to Grand Rapids to meet me. With four years between us, Danica looked enough like me for folks at my church and all over town to wonder if we were sisters. She had a keen sense of humor and a natural "aunt quality" of nurturing and fun.

Later, after supper in the cottage, Danica and I took a walk with the boys to get ice cream. Dora and Bill watched Phoebe. I was touched by Dora's evident love for them all, even Phoebe, who obviously wasn't her biological grandchild. Bill accepted us converging upon his family with quiet grace. When he rocked Phoebe to sleep and gave her a bottle that night, my heart broke. Her real opa should be the one rocking her to sleep, if his arms had not been too chemoravaged to hold her. The incongruity made me ache.

...

As we ambled up the wooded path to the ice cream shack, Danica and I talked about everything but my turmoil. I couldn't have articulated it if I tried. But when we got to the shack, something happened to illuminate the moment.

I spotted a familiar-looking woman around my age, licking her ice cream cone and sitting on a picnic table by the shack. All of a sudden it came to me.

"Are you . . . Tanya? From M.B.C.I?" I asked her.

Tanya and I were casual friends in high school. We had bonded over her dating my stepcousin Willy, the family hottie with piercing blue eyes and white-blond surfer hair.

Taking a few more steps toward the picnic table, I added, "I'm Lori Reimer, or I used to be."

The woman stood up, recognition flashing in her eyes. "Lori! I can't believe it!"

I hadn't seen Tanya in more than twenty years, but I knew that Willy had married someone else. I had left Winnipeg as a college freshman two decades before, so it was startling to run into someone from high school who knew me as spinny, boy-crazy Lori Reimer.

We chatted about kids we used to know and my dreamy cousin Willy. Talk of Willy reminded her of my other stepcousins in the same extended family, whom she had seen earlier in the day.

"You saw them here? Now?" I couldn't believe it. These people had been my family for twenty-five years. I'd spent many hours of my childhood in the basement of North Kildonan Mennonite Brethren Church, attending the wedding receptions of my older stepcousins. We younger cousins would tear around the church together, exploring nooks and crannies after we had squirmed through the *Freiwilliges*, the Mennonite wedding open mic time following the meal.[1] That wonderful church basement smelled permanently of coffee and ham buns, the aroma of a thousand Mennonite weddings steeped into the very baseboards.

I had no idea how much these people meant to me until they were gone.

Actually, *I* left Winnipeg for college at the age of nineteen, and like Anne, I expected everything there to stay the same—all my home-places, rituals, and relatives. I was in for a shock, then, upon learning one Christmas that we no longer gathered together. There had been a rift, growing over the years, between some of my aunts and uncles and their stepsiblings. My dad, ever and always the peacemaker, stayed out of it, other than trying to smooth things over when he could.

Maybe if I lived in Winnipeg, my relationships with my extended family would have continued. But since I came home for only a week or two each year, I had not seen most of my stepcousins in more than a decade.

They were not even relatives through adoption.

Yet as I was reconnecting with Tanya, I had an almost feral urge to find them and claim them. In that strange moment when I felt the Reimer clan stepping back into this reunion with my birth family, a scenario appeared in my mind. I watched myself, clutching my three children, banging on my stepcousins' cottage door, and begging them to take me in. "You're my *real* family," I declared, just before they enfolded me to their cousinly bosom.

And it would be the truest thing.

My heart beat eagerly in my chest, but I knew to act on my impulses would cause deep offense. I couldn't do that to Dora and Danica.

So I smiled at my old friend from high school. "Please tell them all hello from me," I said.

Then I collected my children and some extra napkins, and we made our way back down the beach path, away from my family and toward my flesh-and-blood relatives.

April 2008

I wasn't asked to be Danica's bridesmaid, and I was perfectly fine with that. Her relationship with her close friends was much more long-term than her relationship with me, a quasi sister she had met a few years before. Other than three face-to-face visits—including the beach day two years before—we had conversed mostly via e-mail.

Doyle and I had flown into Calgary for the big day, and we showed up a couple of hours before the wedding to lend a hand. (My chief assignment was to help the indomitable matron of honor, Tova, glue her imposing bosom into the strapless, lavender bridesmaid dress so it would not pop out during the ceremony.)

The sleek bride was a vision in her creamy, mermaid-style gown—her big brown eyes sparkling. I was overjoyed that Danica had found such a good man, an easygoing guy named Cole. It felt important and right to be there, even though our relationship was different from that of most sisters.

My mood was buoyant until we reached the parking lot of the church. Here I was seized with nerves, and my heart beat faster. Was I nervous for Danica? No, she had this. All that was left to do was cheer her and Cole all the way to the "I dos."

As we walked toward the church, Dora grabbed my hand. She was also anxious. Not only was her child getting married, but I sensed that her family dynamics were currently tense, and there was nothing like a wedding to ratchet up the tension. Two of her sisters, Liz and Sharla, were going to be there, having flown in the day before. They brought with them one of her nephews and her mother, my birth

Aunt Sharla, with a voice as whispery as a dove, was the first to take an ice pick to the glacier of gaucheness that was this situation.

"Hi," she said in honeyed vapors, offering her little hand. "I'm your aunt Sharla."

"Wow! Hi!"

I'll spare you. Suffice to say that there were many pleased utterances featuring exclamation marks at the end of them.

A few feet behind her, other assorted relatives lurked, beaming. Aunt Sharla's husband was next, followed by their son, my cousin, a congenial hockey ref who vaguely looked like Ezra, but maybe that was the power of suggestion.

But there was no power of suggestion behind the fact that Uncle Vic had Ezra's nose. Vic was the most relaxed of all the relatives, a friendly, good-looking guy with entrepreneurial zest. We chatted about his current venture: gold prospecting. For a moment, my keyed-up shoulders began to relax, and I started to breathe normally again. See! This whole Meet the Bios isn't as bad as I thought. Except it felt pretty weird.

Anne never had a moment quite like this one. But I realized that someone else in Maud's books had. In fact, as meetings with one's kin go, mine wasn't nearly as bad as Emily's in *Emily of New Moon*, my second-favorite of Maud's literary heroines.

In the first book of the Emily trilogy, we meet dear Emily, a softer, more introspective girl than Anne, with a sharply focused passion for writing. She, too, was orphaned, although she had been raised by a father who adored and understood her. When Douglas Starr died, leaving young Emily at the mercy of her dead mother's estranged people, she was thoroughly daunted by the vaunted Murrays of New Moon.

The first meeting did not go well.

"Emily walked rigidly downstairs before Ellen and into the parlor.

Eight people were sitting around it—and she instantly felt the critical gaze of sixteen stranger eyes."

The introductions begin: "This is your Uncle Wallace. . . . Your Aunt Eva."[2]

Uncle Oliver. Aunt Addie. Terrifying Aunt Ruth. Formidable Aunt Elizabeth. And then, lovely Aunt Laura and Cousin Jimmy.

"[Emily] felt deserted. . . . She was alone now before the bar of Murray opinion. She would have given anything to be out of the room. Yet in the back of her mind a design was forming of writing all about it. . . . She could describe them all—she knew she could."[3]

As Aunt Elizabeth gazed at her niece, she thought of Emily as "alien," but the girl was no more space invader to them than they were to her. But Emily knew that writing about it all would make it so much more manageable. "Courage and hope flooded her cold little soul like a wave of rosy light."[4]

Unfortunately, no such design occurred to me there at the country club in Calgary. Emily of New Moon would resort to hiding under the table to get a bead on her new bio relatives; I was tempted to do the same, but it was too late.

"Lori, dear, I've placed you beside Grandma!" Dora chirped brightly. The crowd dispersed.

Oh dear, sweet mother of pearl . . .

Grandma. My mind flashed to my darling grandma Loewen, someone I had loved with my whole heart and who had loved me as wholly as anyone. My grandma, a wheat farmer's wife who dressed her still-peppery hair in a bun until her death at ninety-three, wore dresses and flowery, vintage aprons from cradle to grave, in the Mennonite way. Did she ever wear pants, even when she was bringing in the sheaves alongside my grandpa all those harvest seasons? I think not.

In that flare of memory, I saw my grandma's doe eyes light up at the sight of me on her farmhouse threshold. She had been gone for twelve years, and I missed her. She had deepened and elevated my life with her devotion and care, while this lady next to me, a key provider of my inherited traits, was a stranger.

I knew some of this stranger's back story. Born and raised in the Netherlands, Ketty had been swept off her feet by a soldier from Canada who had been among the heralded troops who liberated the Dutch from Nazi occupation. Steve and his fellow soldiers had freed her (and so many others) from war and starvation. She must have been lightheaded by those "Johnny Canucks," so handsome in their uniforms, true heroes. Finally, there was food to eat in place of tulip bulbs and tree bark, and peace and relief to consume in place of gnawing fear and terror. Who knows what that girl saw and heard during the war years? Who knows what she experienced?

Ketty was pregnant with my birth mother before she even landed in Nova Scotia as one of Canada's earliest Dutch war brides. But here was another broken fairy tale in the branches of my family tree. As it was told to me, Ketty and Steve's love story was a hothouse orchid, unable to withstand the elements of homesickness and a life an ocean away from home. But they were devout Catholics, so my birth grandparents divorced only after many years of marriage.

I had been told that Ketty's relationship with Dora, her eldest daughter, was often a difficult one. Whatever the reasons, their relationship was in ruins when Dora became pregnant with me, when she needed a mother's love most of all.

As I took my seat next to a little old lady with a fuzzy helmet of dyed brown hair, I was a bowl of mixed nuts (and feelings). A burst of raw allegiance kicked in, and I felt a stab of guilt. Was I somehow cheating on Grandma Loewen?

Luckily, one of my spiritual gifts is small talk, and if living in

Grand Rapids for fourteen years had taught me anything, it had taught me how to make small talk with Dutch people.

I sawed into my chicken entrée with gusto. Most people can't eat a bite when they are emotionally taxed, but not me. I wasn't counting calories as I prattled on about every Dutch subject I could think of.

Tulips? Check.

Banket? Check. (Banket, for the uninitiated, is a stick of pastry featuring almond paste—a baked good precious to the heart of Hollanders everywhere.)

Windmills? Those gigantic mints the size of antacid tablets with Queen Wilhelmina's face etched on them? Check!

No Dutch subject was left unturned. Was she a FIFA fan? Speed skating? Boy, those Dutch skaters sure cut a fine figure in those orange suits, eh? As I thumbed through my Dutch Rolodex, Ketty seemed almost nonchalant about meeting me, as if she could take or leave the chance to interact with the grandchild she had never met. She smiled slightly as she talked about her upbringing in the Netherlands and responded to my comments and questions with short answers.

There had been murmurs that maybe Grandma Ketty was slipping a bit. Was that it, or was she truly blasé? Whichever, I found her casual attitude, especially the way she did not gawp at me as if I were the eighth wonder of the world, to be wildly refreshing.

Unfortunately, Ketty's stance was in sharp contrast to others at the table. A friend of Dora's was agog at the astonishing resemblance between me and Ketty. (Boy, nothing strokes the old ego like being told you look exactly like an eighty-year-old woman.)

"It's *amazing*," she oozed. "You two could be *twins*."

Twins? Perfect.

I was saved a time or two by Tova, seated a few feet away at the head table. Every time we made eye contact, she grinned and gave me a thumbs-up to indicate that she and her gown were glued together as one. For this, I will never stop loving her.

Finally, just as I was about to run out of Dutch topics, it was blessedly time for speeches and toasts.

Dora's speech was quiet and subdued. She welcomed Cole to the family and thanked those who had come from out of town, "especially Danica's sister, Lori, who came from Michigan."

Since half the crowd (at least) didn't have a hot clue that Danica had a sister, there was a murmur heard throughout the room. I suppressed the urge to rise and give a wave all round. You could almost hear the puzzle pieces being locked into place as folks figured out that—aha!—that gal in the red dress, the one who looks suspiciously like Danica and is sitting beside Danica's grandmother at a table with Danica's parents, was her, that's who! Because no one can resist an *Oprah* moment.

On the outside, I looked as if all my wits were collected nicely in bins from the Container Store.

Sorted out, as the Brits say.

Pepino suave, as the Spanish say.

However, I was as ruffled as a tutu. My wits were not sorted, but rather strewn willy-nilly all over my humanity like something off a TV show about hoarders. Cool as a cucumber? No sir, Señor Suave. Fried pickle at the fair was more like it.

Fortunately, the guests' attention was soon focused back where it belonged as the bridal party continued its loving, tearful tributes to the bride and groom, who had found each other after a relatively long and winding path. One of my favorites was from Tova, who gave a sweet speech about her decades of friendship with Danica. Then there were toasts and glasses raised to Danica and Cole with hopes for a blessed union of souls.

And then . . . there was dancing.

Now, Mennonites do not partake of dancing at their weddings, at least they didn't when I got hitched to Doyle in 1991. Somehow, *Freiwilleges* stood in for dancing and toasting. Nor do they taste the fruit of the vine. In fact, my dad vetoed the liqueur-laced chocolate cheesecake I had wanted for the "bride's favorite dessert" portion of our wedding menu. My pleas that the alcohol is cooked off in the baking process, that there was no possible way for a guest to become inebriated on a slice of cheesecake, fell on deaf ears. The cheesecake was delicious but decidedly unlaced with any *funny business*.

("We got in *just* under the wire," my mum likes to say about the fact that my Big Fat Mennonite Wedding was one of the last to feature no alcohol or dancing. She says this in the well-satisfied manner of one who has escaped tremendous debauchery. In addition to the ban on dancing and drinking, she would include strapless wedding dresses under this tally. My mum and Anne are on the same page on the subject of puffed sleeves. Anne approves of them because they are the height of fashion, and my mum approves of them because they provide outstanding coverage. When my cousin Jennifer got married eight years after I did, my mother did not mind *one iota* about the DJ, the champagne toasts, or Jen's strapless gown. As for her and her house, *they* had gotten in under the wire.)

Despite this upbringing, or maybe because of it, I love dancing. In fact, about a year before the wedding, Doyle and I had taken seven months of ballroom dancing lessons at Arthur Murray. "What you have here are a Mennonite and a Baptist," I warned our adorable teacher, Mr. Peck. "That's five hundred years of no dancing." To be honest, this dance-free heritage showed. But there was one dance at which we excelled: the Hustle.

I revere the Hustle, because not only is it done to the luscious beats of the 1970s, it also takes on a life of its own once underway, like an amusement park ride. Once you get in the pocket of a fine piece of music such as "Le Freak" by Chic, the Hustle almost dances itself.

On Danica's wedding night, nothing could have provided a better escape than a little disco fever. We were in the pocket of the song, hustling and twirling. This activity beat the pants off of skulking in a bathroom stall.

My bio relatives were also on the dance floor, going to town. Even Ketty was bop/shuffling around the floor. We exchanged smiles as I flew by her.

While I twirled, I sorted wits. These people were a small part of me, and I was a small part of them. Grandma Ketty was more than simply a nice Dutch lady I sat next to at a wedding, listening to her story. But her part was also small. This lady would never claim a stake in my heart, as my grandma Loewen and oma Reimer had. But tonight was our one chance to meet, and I was glad, after all, that Dora had pushed it. I would never see her again.

Exhilarated and sweaty, the dancing duo of Doyle and I left the dance floor and collapsed into chairs. I was relieved the night was coming to a close and that it hadn't been all confusion.

I had seen my birth sister, whom I love, marry a wonderful man. I had made a few new friends, and they, too, fancied dancing. I had learned some things about Ketty's story, and therefore my own story.

Nobody was forcing me to move to an atoll in the sea with these people, forsaking my own loved ones and expunging them from my memory and heart. I could take the meat from these encounters and leave the bones.

As a fairy tale, this one was cracked, true; but as a reunion, it was all starting to make some sense. No, my story probably never would have made it on *Oprah*, but the experience did help connect the dots in a way I hadn't anticipated. Having the chance to integrate my two identities was more of a gift than a burden, and I suddenly felt grateful.

Alles gut, Grandma Loewen used to always say. *Everything is okay. Everything is good. I love you.*

Sometimes when I miss her and can't quite ring her up, I'll throw a roast in the slow cooker, and the smell helps me remember. I never smell roast beef baking without having the memory of her love and nurture. In season, I'll buy a bunch of gladioli, her favorite flower, in peach or deep red, and dunk them in a vase on my kitchen table. I'll wrap myself up in the pink comforter cover she made for me when I went away to college until I can feel her again.

She is with me still. She is my grandma always. I hold her everywhere, even at the table at a wedding reception where an old Dutch war bride sits next to me.

Alles gut, Grandma. I love you too, forever.

Raspberry Cordial and Redemption in a Bottle of Ipecac Syrup

God is in the salvage business . . . salvaging our lives, making use of every scrap we offer, even turning our wounds and our failings into the tools of his gracious repair.

DEB RIENSTRA, *SO MUCH MORE*

THERE WAS NO RASPBERRY CORDIAL on offer at Danica and Cole's wedding that April day in Calgary (or at my wedding either, for that matter), but oh, what a superb beverage! Since I started whipping up my own raspberry cordial, I've learned it's a crucial matter of setting a timer, because as my dear husband has mentioned (carefully), foods that require attending are not my best gifts to the culinary world. (I invoke Anne, who *meant* to cover the plum pudding sauce but unfortunately got carried away in a daydream, whereupon a wayfaring mouse fell in the pitcher and met his end.[1])

Here's the recipe, kind of: Dump two bags of frozen raspberries in a pan. (It doesn't make that much difference whether you thaw them first.) Chase that with a cup and a quarter of sugar, and set the pan on medium heat. Set the timer for fifteen minutes, but don't go far (and by far, I mean don't go upstairs to your computer and become snagged on watching cat videos on the Internet). Really, it's safer to just stay in the kitchen the whole time.

Meanwhile, in a separate pot, boil six cups of water. When the sugar is melted, turn off the heat and mash the berries to smithereens with a potato masher. (Don't wear your new white sweater.)

Phoebe likes to squeeze the smithereens out of two lemons, which we reserve in a small bowl. The hardest part is straining the berries and sugar into a bowl, but even that isn't all that hard. Pour the boiling water over the whole thing, and let it chill for a few hours (or not), and voilà! You have made a divinely scrumptious Victorian brew that will help you win friends and influence people—it really will. No one can resist real raspberry cordial, a zingy, fruity master-work that distills the very soul of the berry. Even the zesty hot pink/red color adds to the overall effect of festivity and cheer. Leave it to Anne to point that out: "I love bright red drinks, don't you? They taste twice as good as any other color."[2]

Mix in your favorite sparkling beverage, or leave it as is. Use your best golden lusterware cups from your Grandma's china cabinet, or break out the Dixie cups. Either way, serve it with *joie de vivre* in the company of kindred spirits. It's the way Anne would want it to be.

Just don't pour tumblers full of this nectar to folks who think it's merely "juice." Anne wouldn't approve. It's no ordinary pour, this drink that Anne thought she was serving Diana on the fateful day her bosom friend came for tea. *Cordial* infers that this is a convivial drink, good for the heart—a drink of friendship. Raspberry cordial is extra-ordinary; it has powers to revive, invigorate, and hearten, just like the winds off Four Winds Harbor, just like the power of redemption after a big misunderstanding.

...

The Raspberry Cordial Episode is one of my best-loved stories in the book, not only for its great charm, sparkle, and fizz at the beginning, but for the way it demonstrates the mighty, unshakable power of redemption. It's really a story of reclamation in three distinct acts.

The first act is all froth and fun; we readers get to revel in Anne's exuberance, her ever-more-satisfying friendship with Diana, and their *plumb adorable* plans for a tea party. We witness Anne Shirley, jumping out of her skin, more "addlepated" than ever, according to Marilla.[3] She was just so excited that she was being allowed to entertain Diana, on her own, as a formal guest to Green Gables! There would be cherry preserves on offer, as well as fruitcake and snaps. The pièce de résistance, the menu item sending Anne through the roof, was the half bottle of raspberry cordial, left over from the church social and sitting on the second shelf of the sitting-room closet. Except of course, things were not what they seemed, which they never are in cases of wild misunderstanding.

Yes, things were positively delightful at their tea—until Anne brought out the raspberry cordial. Then events began to spiral wildly out of control.

Soon Diana had consumed three tumblers full and declared it *the nicest* raspberry cordial she ever drank! We all know what happens next: Diana accidentally became drunk, boiled as an owl, hooched-up, pie-eyed, sauced, snockered, and spiffed, and then lurched home in this condition to her pinched mother. Anne wondered if Diana was coming down with smallpox, offering to care for her if only she'd stay for tea, but such was not the case.

Nothing prepares Marilla for the news that Diana Barry, age eleven, had been *set drunk* in her parlor—"Drunk fiddlesticks!" she averred.[4] At first Marilla didn't believe it, until it dawned on her that she had put the bottle of cordial in the cellar instead of in the pantry. Anne had mistakenly nabbed a bottle of her famous red currant wine—famous and illicit. At the time Maud wrote Anne's story,

PEI was a dry island under a prohibition law, and Marilla's mulled wine would have been illegal. People such as Mrs. Barry would have frowned upon it anyway, although Mrs. Barry frowned upon almost everything. (We don't know Mrs. Barry's first name, nor do we ever want to know it.)

Mrs. Barry *can* be excused for being upset at the sight of her unworldly daughter, sullied with drunkenness at age eleven. What's sad—well, the first sad thing—was that she believed Anne had gotten Diana drunk out of malice—our kind, openhearted Anne! Again, the distrust for the orphan rises like smog.

Her face hard, and her anger of the surly, stony sort that is always hardest to overcome, a scowling Mrs. Barry banished Anne from Diana's friendship for life. (And here we all grimace in sympathy and clench our teeth. Onlookers observing our reading: Look away! Whatever expression we have on our faces as we read, it ain't pretty.)

"I don't think you are a fit little girl for Diana to associate with," Mrs. Barry proclaimed.[5] Once again, our hearts break, because Anne heard that she's not suitable, acceptable, good enough, *enough*. Mrs. Barry might have exiled Anne from being loved—that's what this ousting must have felt like. And it was all based on a mix-up, which doesn't actually surprise me.

The thing is, mix-ups happen. We long to be known and understood as we are—wholly, utterly—but the problem is we live in a damaged world. Misjudging each other will always happen, and hurt and mess will always ensue. Sometimes the tangles can be unpicked with an apology, but not always. Often, as is evidenced in the case of Anne and the cordial/currant wine, these misunderstandings result in our most hidden wound—the one that says we're not worthy—getting thumped again.

A few years ago, a wheel came off my friendship with another writer. By wheel coming off, I mean we were driving down the highway at seventy miles per hour when that thing flew off, leaving scorched road and curls of burnt rubber for miles. I'll spare you the gory details, but the short story is that she became much more famous than I about six months after we became friends, and that was the beginning of the end.

I've told you about my Guild—the most supportive and encouraging community of writers a girl could ask for. Any one of us would do anything for another, including donating organs and repeating praiseworthy things about each other at top volume in front of random editors and agents.

In my mind, this new writer friend was an extension of them. As it turned out, she wasn't—not even close.

Here's what happened: An editor I was working with on a book idea told me that if I was able to secure an endorsement from my friend, it would give my proposal a big boost. I saw no reason at all why I couldn't ask her for one.

Ugh. Double, triple *ugh.* As I mentioned, this story is headed down a bad road with charred rubber and bits of smoking metal. When I casually asked her about the blurb one night over dinner, this friend—always so generous and encouraging—went cold. You could see your breath in the freezing air as she began to articulate why an endorsement from her would be a problem. The upshot? I simply was not belletristic or "literary" enough for her. (Belletristic: basically, "literary," so apparently she deemed me doubly unliterary.) Moreover, her endorsement was, apparently, a "precious gift to be used wisely." I listened in shock and horror, hardly believing my ears. I barely knew what to say and answered as politely as I could before grabbing the check and making my exit. When I got home, I prayed the best prayer for when you are blindsided and confused: "Help."

About a month later, my heart made pliable by many prayers, I tried to make amends via e-mail (never a good idea, even for a writer). Despite my humiliation and hurt, I missed her, and I worried about her because I knew she'd been battling some health issues. I apologized for making her feel awkward, for assuming too much, asking too much. Had my motives been mixed as her star rose in the literary world? Maybe a little, I confessed, but I knew for sure that hadn't been my main motive. The blurb didn't matter, but her friendship did.

My words were imperfect and probably made things worse. All I know is, things started to get really weird. Her reply scalded me further with accusations of using her from the beginning. She concluded her two-page, belletristic diatribe with the directive that, should we ever run into each other at say, a writer's conference, we would pass each other by, not speaking, mind you, but with the thought, *Ah, there goes a writer with a very different vision than I.* I took her words to mean: *Don't even look at me. I don't think you are a fit person for me to associate with.* The earth between us was slashed and burned. She was Lord Kitchener; I was the Boers. She was the Russian army; I was Napoleon. She was Sherman; I was—you get the picture. Years later, it's hard for me to believe this really happened. But mix-ups happen, alright, much as we wish they wouldn't. The bigger question is what happens after the crashing and burning? Will there be beauty for ashes?

...

Redemption is not always obvious. Not at all. We are often blinded to the ways in which our adoptive Father swaps our wrecking balls for His renovation projects. If only we opened our eyes to see. If only we remembered that even in the dark, in the silence, He is working, salvaging our junkyard scraps, saving us forever.

As for Anne, the first redemptive hint readers see in the raspberry cordial debacle was between acts, so to speak. It came from Marilla, who was surely awakening under the influence of her orphan surprise. In the aftermath of Anne's latest scrape, the spinster's mama heart was stirred by the sight of her girl's tearstained, sleeping face, causing her own hard face to soften.

"Poor little soul," she murmured, lifting a loose curl of hair from the child's tearstained face. Then she bent down and kissed the flushed cheek on the pillow.[6]

A buried part of Marilla Cuthbert's humanity emerged like an olive sprout out of scorched earth—a sign that all things were being made new.

...

"All things great are wound up with all things little," Maud begins chapter 18,[7] and indeed no less than Sir John A. Macdonald, Canada's first prime minister, looms large in act 2 and her plot to initiate Anne's deliverance.

On the night of rescue and redemption, Marilla was off gadding with Rachel Lynde at a political meeting in Charlottetown, where the premier (thought to represent Sir John A.) was holding forth. So Anne and Matthew had the place all to themselves on this cozy, sleepy January evening. They were having the sweetest conversation about geometry, politics, and what makes PEI roads red when the last person they were expecting burst through the door in desperate need of help.

Diana begged Anne to come with her to help save her three-year-old sister, Minnie Mae, who had suddenly experienced a terrifying acceleration in croup and was nearly choking to death. Anne and Diana raced across the snow to the Barry house as Matthew set off to alert the doctor. Diana and Anne found Minnie Mae badly off, choking and gasping. Things looked grim. But Anne hadn't brought up three sets of twins in Mrs. Hammond's household for nothing. As the night ticked by in agony, Anne brought crucial knowledge and focus (for once) to the situation. She administered doses of ipecac syrup until the danger had passed. (Ipecac: This expectorant [mucous expeller] and emetic [vomit inducer] was once used as a heavy duty cough syrup and antidote to poisoning.)

We know what happens next: Anne saved Minnie Mae! Mrs. Barry could do nothing but throw herself at Anne's feet in remorse and gratitude, restoring Anne to her good graces and to her daughter's friendship.

This drives me crazy.

While I'm glad poor little Minnie Mae was spared and that Anne's true colors were revealed and her kindred spirit restored, this scene has always bugged me. Why did it have to take Anne *saving a life* for Mrs. Barry to see the light? Wasn't there a less drastic way for Anne to earn her mercy? Mrs. Barry's forgiveness doesn't feel like grace; it was so grudgingly given.

Unfortunately, in Mrs. Barry's stiff-necked posture, I see my frequent inability to give an inch when I feel wronged. I see those who have hurt me. I see my own mulish soul.

From our human vantage point, there isn't always an antidote to the poison. There may not be a way to save relationships choking to death. Too often, love wastes away on the vine of unforgiveness.

But from the Redeemer's position, mercy and favor are stronger forces than all our wreckage and rubble. There are grace notes everywhere, if you have ears to hear them.

...

In Avonlea's parlance, the new minister's wife was a perfect duck, and for Maud's literary purposes, she was an agent of grace and a vehicle of redemption. For me, act 3 of the raspberry cordial saga is one of the book's treasures and a reason why *Anne of Green Gables* is so beloved.

We are not told Mrs. Allan's first name, but in this case, we wish we knew it. Like Anne, we fall completely in love with the new Sunday school teacher, a smiling, laughing creature open to the endless questions of the red-haired magpie in her class.

We can almost sense through the pages the bustle of nervous preparation when Reverend and Mrs. Allan were invited to Green Gables for tea. Apparently, it was not any old day that the minister and wife were had to tea; this was a serious responsibility and undertaking. The stakes were high—do we really feel nervous on Anne's behalf? Yes!—and we empathize with Anne as she strove to please her new kindred spirit with gorgeous food and table decor.

Go back and read the menu if you haven't in a while. It makes me feel full just by reading it: jellied chicken and cold tongue (because every minister should be treated to cold tongue); red and yellow jelly; whipped cream and lemon pie and cherry pie; three kinds of cookies; fruit cake; Marilla's famous yellow plum preserves, kept especially for ministers; pound cake; baking powder biscuits; and new bread and old[8] in case the minister is dyspeptic (because new bread might have too much yeast in it, as if eating for twelve wouldn't cause dyspepsia). Laws! Were they planning to remove the Allans by rolling them out the door?

The layer cake was the sixteenth item on the menu, baked by Anne herself as the crowning glory of this feast. It was passed around the table last, and kindly Mrs. Allan, though she had been stuffed within an inch of her life, sampled it because she knew it was made with great tender care.

For what comes next, I honor this lady. With one bite of Anne's cake, Mrs. Allan knew something was drastically amiss. Anne had accidentally flavored the cake with liniment, Avonlea's version of Vicks VapoRub. It was another pantry mix-up, another opportunity for the offended one to choose resentment or compassion. Depending on the offended one's choice, each person around the table would be taken down the road to perdition or on the road to grace. Thankfully for Anne, the minister's wife was a frequent traveler down the latter.

Mrs. Allan, you are a perfect duck! Everyone should have a Mrs. Allan in their lives, someone who accepts our tainted offerings and believes in us anyway. She still said yes to Anne, though it cost her. She was still for Anne. Like our Father, Mrs. Allan pursued Anne when she ran away in shame and disgrace. She followed her, listened with a heart full of mercy, and regarded Anne's tragic face with deep concern. Her compassion bore the image of God.

Mrs. Allan saw Anne's brokenness, not as something to be shamed, but as a wound to carefully anoint and bind up. In those forgiving eyes, the orphan girl was more than her messes—Anne was a whole person with a marvelous gift of bringing star-shine to a cloud-covered world. We learn volumes from this loving character about how we can also be agents of grace and vehicles of redemption.

We lean forward as Mrs. Allan guided Anne in repair: "I assure you I appreciate your kindness and thoughtfulness just as much as if it had turned out all right. Now, you mustn't cry any more, but come down with me and show me your flower garden."[9] ("Do not call to mind the former things, or ponder things of the past" [Isaiah 43:18].)

She helped Anne move on, which can be the greatest medicine—liniment for a sore spirit. We wonder how we can repair damage in our world, how we can guide our daughters and sons.

Mulled wine for cordial, liniment for vanilla, mistakes for good intentions—these all speak to our cracked condition. Thank heaven for act 3, for redemption. It renovates and innovates, creating treasure from our trashy offerings.

No doubt at all, there will always be damage and damage doers. I will do damage today, probably. So I'm obliged for the possibility of repair. As Doyle and I have read about adoption and parenting an adopted child, we've grabbed hold of the idea of discipline being different from punishment. Instead of sending our girl to her room (banishing her again!) for some damage she's created, we try to think of ways in which we can guide her in repairing the situation. This is not the easy path, but involving her in her own mending, her own restoration, is a powerful thing.

On this side of life, we live at least partially in the ruins, but as Mrs. Barry and Mrs. Allan show us, we also have a choice: to make things messier, more ruinous, or to roll up our sleeves and join in the reclamation.

And those grace notes I mentioned earlier? They aren't that hard to discern, even here, even in the ruins: I see *salvage* in a growing number of Korean pastors who are challenging ancient culture and advocating for orphans in their distress. I see *restoration* in Lee Jong-rak, who made a Baby Box, a heated drop box lined in soft towels to receive otherwise abandoned babies on the streets of Seoul. Eighteen babies per month are surrendered to the box, which has a bell in it that alerts Lee, his wife, and volunteers to go scoop up the priceless bundle and bring him or her inside.[10] As Lee collects babies, this restorer is bearing the image of the One who trades desperation for hope.

Sometimes the repair work is invisible, with no noticeable clues. In the case of my former writer friend, I may never lay eyes on her again, but I came to a place a long time ago of peace and wishing her well. Knowing her as I did, I would like to believe she abides in the same restful spot. Someday, we will get a chance to compare notes, although that day might come on the other side. And that's okay.

I'd like to propose a toast, then, to friendship and compassion— and when failing at those things, to redemption. Our Father's specialty is taking our tuneless offerings and transposing them into new songs.

Let's raise our glasses of raspberry cordial to the kindred spirits of this world, to the Mrs. Allans and Lee Jong-raks, to restorers who receive our cracked places with mercy. They help us belong to each other. And while we're at it, let's keep our glasses raised for one more toast, to those who snub us, hurt us, and abandon us in our time of need.

May this drink of friendship revive us, oh Lord. May it be as a cup of cold water in Your name.

Finding Walter Shirley

My two parents represent the single greatest influence on my life. And if my dad
had been there for me, it would be the double greatest influence on my life.

JAROD KINTZ

THERE IS ONE STORY IN THE ANNE SERIES that breaks my heart more
than any other. It hits too close to home. I have so much to celebrate
in my life—but there's one thing Anne Shirley found that I never
have. When she knocked on the door of the run-down yellow house
in which she had been born, Anne was embarking on a quest to find
the human father who would never fail her. A very tall, thin woman
answered the door.

Our Anne was on a weekend visit to her college roommate's home
(remember the superbly wacky Philippa Gordon, aka "Phil"?). This
"sojourn,"[1] as *Anne of the Island* puts it, would be remembered for
Anne's pilgrimage to her birthplace. Here she would find her roots as
the daughter of Bertha and Walter Shirley, a man who, she was going
to find out quickly, had her exact carotene shade of hair.

As it turned out, the woman at the door did remember the Shirleys:

"Yes, the Shirleys lived here twenty years ago," she said, in answer to
Anne's question. "They had it rented. I remember 'em. They both died

of fever at onct. It was turrible sad. They left a baby. I guess it's dead long ago. It was a sickly thing. . . ."

"It didn't die," said Anne, smiling. "I was that baby." ["It"? *Oh, 1885!*]

"You don't say so! Why, you have grown," exclaimed the woman, as if she were much surprised that Anne was not still a baby. "Come to look at you, I see the resemblance. You're complected like your pa. He had red hair. But you favor your ma in your eyes and mouth."[2]

The tall, thin woman, though she might not have been the brightest light in the harbor, possessed a good, kind heart, and obliged when Anne eagerly asked to roam the house of her birth.

"Laws, yes, you can if you like."[3] Then the woman ushered Anne into the very room where Bertha had given birth, and outside of which Walter had no doubt paced anxiously. Afterward the tall, thin woman left Anne alone to commune with ghosts who had inhabited the space of life and death, happiness and despair. It was for Anne, "one of the jeweled hours of life that gleam out radiantly forever in memory."[4]

I find it fascinating that Maud granted Anne this jeweled hour, the crowning moment of an orphan's quest to piece together her fragmented beginnings. She gave Anne the chance to meet her parents, Bertha and the "sorter homely"[5] Walter. (You've got to hand it to the tall, thin lady. She wasn't afraid to lay it all out on the table. *Yeah, I remember your dad. Great guy, but kinda ugly.*)

Like a fairy godmother, Maud bestowed upon her Book Child clues on the breadcrumb path to finding her original family— a packet of letters tied in blue ribbon, and a visit to the grave in which both her parents lay.

Of course, when the tall, thin woman offered Anne the letters her parents had written each other, she took them, "clasping the packet rapturously."[6] Our Anne Girl couldn't merely *hold* such a packet.

Clutching the letters, Anne made a beeline from the shabby yellow house to the Bolingbroke cemetery, where, said the tall, thin woman, the school board had put up a tombstone to Walter and Shirley as a reward for faithful service. Their daughter paid homage, placing a bouquet of white flowers on the single grave.

In the packet of letters, Anne found that her parents had loved each other and her dearly.

At their grave, she discovered that her original parents had existed—here was proof etched in stone.

Many orphans never get the chance to discover such proof of their original family's actuality. Most don't come to the end of their searches to find evidence that they had been dearly loved. Generally, we find out the opposite was true. But Maud wanted a different outcome for Anne than she herself had received.

Maud, starved for a father's love, gave Anne not only Matthew Cuthbert, but also Walter Shirley. Good, loving, homely Walter Shirley would have been an exceptionally attentive and warmhearted dad, but of course he died, so he *couldn't* be there for his daughter in a million different ways. Meanwhile, Monty Montgomery, Maud's father, was very much alive. But he *wouldn't* be there for his child, in a million different ways.

The orphan's heart knows this very well: There's a big difference between couldn't and wouldn't.

. . .

"Do you know anything about Phoebe's real dad?" is one comment that grates me like a cheese shredder.

When people say this—and they do with shocking regularity—I am thankful for forty-plus years of socialization. Also, normally there are no brooms handy with which to begin beating these people.

Oh, I understand what they are saying. They mean, do we know anything about her biological father, the source of half our daughter's genes, the guy whose unremarkable and fleeting romance resulted in our extraordinary, permanent girl?

Obviously, calling a birth father "real" is wildly inaccurate. They are typically somewhat vaporous beings, absent, missing, and fictional in one's imagination. At this point, the man in the moon is just as much Phoebe's real father as the one who donated his genetic material.

But . . .

After forty-five years of thinking about my own birth father—or not thinking of him, as was usually the case—I know this for sure now: Phoebe's first father *is* actually important to her spirit and sense of identity. Sure, for all tangible intents the man is lost to her, probably forever. The fact that his ancestral code is zigzagging inside my child means he is with her day to day—a part of her. Should Phoebe ever get to meet Moon, I know she'll have lots of questions about her chromosomal padre: What was he like? Was he handsome? Funny? Do I look like him? Was he good at soccer? Did he play goalie, like me? What did you mean when you said he wasn't the person you thought he was?

I'll be eager for the answers, especially to the last question. What did you mean, Moon, when you were answering the social worker's questions? What did you say to the social worker to make her jot this down: "He wasn't the person she hoped he would be"? Did Moon even say it like that, or was it hopelessly lost in translation?

The Mart Worker of Seoul, South Korea

On our trip to pick up our six-and-a-half-month-old daughter in Seoul, I would scan the faces of Korean men, looking for my child in their golden skin and marquise-shaped eyes. "She has double eyelids!" Koreans would tell us with great gusts of enthusiasm, exulting over this prized feature in Phoebe's face. This was confusing to us, of course, being Caucasian. We had never before contemplated or counted our own eyelids or anyone else's. (I just now counted my eyelids and regret doing so. Don't count your eyelids if you are over forty.)

I discovered later that for women and girls of Asian descent, especially Koreans, having double eyelids can increase your beauty by twofold—or at least that's what they are told from a young age by their parents, friends, and culture. It's no wonder blepharoplasty, or double-eyelid surgery, is a common practice for many young Asian girls. One in *five* Korean girls undergoes this surgery, also a popular graduation present from parents.

Did Phoebe get her eyes and their cherished extra creases from her birth father?

Surely, this fellow was a looker, because baby Eun Jung Kim, soon to be Phoebe Min-Ju-Jayne Craker, was so beautiful.

Surely, if he had his life together a little more and had understood what he was giving up, he wouldn't have left Moon and her baby.

Some might argue that "Hey!—he was only twenty-one or twenty-two, unable to step up and be a man, right? Cut the dude some slack, lady." But that argument seems about as offbeat as giving your daughter an extra pair of eyelids for graduation—what, the stores were all out of watches and mini-fridges? (Although I can't really judge because we North Americans do some pretty nutty things to meet our own idealized standards for beauty. Hello, hand lifts!) I think of my wonderful nephew, Jake, who became a father at twenty-one. Too young, most would say. Yet Jake is a straight arrow. I know he will be stepping up and shooting straight for the next eighteen years and beyond for his blue-eyed, chubby-cheeked baby boy.

In Seoul, I was in search of a crooked arrow, not a straight one. One tidbit revealed by the adoption paperwork was that the bio father and mother had worked together in a "mart." So I was drawn to marts during our trip (not to mention the fact that they were a blast of frigid air in Seoul, which was draped in humidity like a wet sleeping bag). I would find excuses to duck in and buy a bag of chips or a can of cold iced green tea. The cozy marts smelled cool and spicy, like green tea and ginseng, kimchi and sesame oil. They held all manner of otherworldly snacks and beverages that intrigued us to no end.

Once, Doyle grabbed a small can of something called Pine Tree Drink, decorated with emerald pine branches and the Hangul alphabet characters, and I sipped it delicately. The taste reminded me of disinfectant fumes, but Doyle swigged the whole can to my amazement. "I kind of like it," he said.

In the city of Pine Tree Drink, I scanned thousands of beautiful Korean faces, never recognizing the strangers whose union gave us our daughter. I still scan people's faces now, when I see them out and about or on TV. Fun fact: Because Los Angeles has the highest concentration of Koreans in North America, the majority of Asian actors you see on-screen are Korean. This gives me license to make stuff up, like Phoebe's birth father could be Daniel Dae Kim from *Lost*! Well, almost certainly not.

Whoever he is, I hope he's got his life together now. Maybe he went back to school and is now performing meaningful work in a job he loves (like as an actor on *Lost* and *Hawaii Five-O*!). Mostly, I hope he is growing into a man Phoebe could someday be proud of, a man who shows that actions are more important than words.

I'm betting Phoebe won't waste much time wondering who he is until she's older. It's hard enough to wrap your mind around the fact that there is someone out there, not the person you call "mama," in whose belly you grew, knitted together by an unseen hand. There's a much stronger link with her.

Phoebe could strongly favor her birth father in looks, personality, and abilities, but he will be more abstract to her than an unseen planet. At least she'll be taught about the planet in school, whereas no one outside of us will teach her about that imaginary pater, a black hole, her first dad.

About the only piece of information we can give her about this guy, apart from his age and his mart work, is Moon's remark, swathed in questions.

He wasn't the person I hoped he would be.

Oh, how I wish I knew what she meant.

I also wish he was the kind of man, even at twenty-one, Moon could have come to with this news, even after they had broken up. True, she could have given him the chance to step up, but she didn't—an echo of my own story. But something tells me she would have given him that chance, if the mart worker hadn't been a crooked arrow with a bent heart, if only he had been the person she hoped he was.

The Jack-of-all-Trades from Prince Edward Island

Only a real dad cares about getting his daughter a string of pearls and a dress with the puffiest of sleeves. Only a genuine father orders a strapping boy to help him with the farm work and loves what he receives instead: a scraggy cockatoo of a girl who never stops twittering. I *adore* Matthew Cuthbert!

Yet it intrigues me that while Maud created one of literature's most devoted fathers, she herself carried a hollow where her own father should have been.

Today a young widowed father would assume full parenting duties, whether or not he eventually remarried. But this was 1876, and when his wife died, the grieving "Monty" deposited his dark-haired baby girl with her maternal grandparents. Unfortunately, Alexander and Lucy Woolner Macneill treated tiny Maud much like Anne was often treated: like a charity case.

Maud's childhood was desperately lonely, and she was never allowed to forget she was living under her grandparents' roof because no one else wanted her. Her grandparents were the sort to force her to kneel on the hard floor and pray for forgiveness for being such a "bad girl." Alexander Macneill mostly ignored Maud, even leaving his daughter's daughter out of his will *on purpose* when he died. (While time traveling, I'd also make a stop in Victorian PEI to administer a tongue lashing upon the Macneills they wouldn't soon forget, *that's what.*)

When Maud was seven, her beloved father deserted her entirely, choosing to move to the humming Wild West town of Prince Albert, Saskatchewan, to make his mark and hopefully his fortune. He left behind a little girl who was lonelier than ever. She was so lonely, Maud's imagination gave rise to two companions living in the oval glass doors of the bookcase: Lucy Gray and Katie Maurice.

Father and daughter wrote letters, but the ties between them grew thinner until he seemed almost as imaginary as her oval glass friends. She pined for her father, and she daydreamed about all the ways in which he would delight in her, should they be reunited. He would laugh at her jokes, admire her poems, and call her "Maudie" in that special way. Life would be beautiful again if only they were together.

So she clasped the letter rapturously when Monty wrote her at age sixteen. Monty had remarried to twenty-seven-year-old Mary Ann, and they had a toddler daughter and a baby on the way. Now that he was settled out west, it was time for Maud to come live with him and complete his family.

Throughout the nearly transcontinental train ride, Maud's heart swelled with hopes and dreams. She was chaperoned by her Montgomery grandfather, a Canadian senator. As they rolled past the leafy farmlands, the craggy rocks of the Canadian Shield, and then the swaying prairie grasses and big skies, Maud could hardly wait to be reunited with her charming dad, a businessman with his fingers in many pies. Getting to know her father better, belonging to him at last, would surely give Maud a sense of permanence. No longer would she feel like a turnip that fell off the back of a truck.

Like so many birth-father fantasies, Maud's went bust soon after arrival in Prince Albert. In her girlish daydreams, there was no room for conditional love or for the young, bossy stepmother who lost no time in working her like a pack mule. In letters home to her cousin, Pensie Macneill, Maud expressed bitter disappointment about the turn of events. She was little more than Mary Ann's unpaid servant, a boomtown Cinderella set to scrubbing floors, wiping noses, and changing diapers. The cruelest blow: For two months she was kept home from school to mop and scour.

Monty, a noodle of a man, would not defend his daughter. Mary Ann was jealous of her teenage stepdaughter and would throw a fit if Monty called Maud "Maudie" in his old, affectionate way. When Maud begged him to intervene, her father threw up his hands.

(Science, where are we at with time travel? Because I'm ready to go, and I'm packing a broom this time.)

After a year, Maud could no longer stand it. Between Monty's spinelessness and Mary Ann's cruelty, her dreams of fitting in were ground down like Saskatchewan prairie dust. She decided to return home.

Crusty grandparents aside, Maud belonged to the Island's red-dirt beaches and purple lupine-lined paths—here was her haven and port. Here she didn't have to face the fact that her father's love was a shadow of her own; that by his own act he had deserted her once and continued to desert her by his choices; that he was not the man she thought him to be.

Coach Tom from Manitoba

I always kind of hoped that Neil Young was my birth father, rooted in the fact that Neil lived in Winnipeg from the age of twelve until he moved away to become a famous rock star. He was the right age, so just doing the math was enough to suggest the possibility that someday he and I could've been reunited, singing "Heart of Gold" and waging heavy peace together.

Things broke down when I roped in Joni Mitchell as my potential birth mother (they *did* meet in smoky Winnipeg clubs in the sixties). The truth is I look less like Joni Mitchell than any human being could possibly look. Case in point: Joni has cheekbones, and the only bone jutting out of my face is my nose. I'm afraid I look more like Neil Young than Joni Mitchell.

When I look back on these fantastical musings, I wonder how I could have ever thought, even in jest, that I issued forth from two musical legends. The highlight of my music career was when a voice teacher at our church cryptically suggested to my mother that my voice might be "teachable." The low point was getting kicked out of seventh-grade band for not turning in my practice sheets. Also a low ebb: when Mr. Duba, my ancient and potbellied clarinet teacher, routinely fell asleep as I played clarinet scales for him. I am many things, but Benny Goodman I am not.

When I was reunited with Dora, she confirmed that there was precious little musical aptitude to be found on her side of the family. Also, artistic ability was meager, though I have always loved to draw and paint and sculpt. I remember finding my dad's fine-pencil sketches of birds one day in a drawer jammed with old papers. When I confronted him with his talent, he was bemused. "That was a long time ago," he said, smiling. In the mysterious alchemy of adoption, could my artistic talents somehow be traced to my dad? Or could art be seeded and encrypted via my birth father?

He—my birth father—wasn't Neil Young, of course, but it was always kind of pleasant to imagine what might have been. When you don't know where you came from, you can and will imagine all kinds of things.

Your original family members are like missing persons no one is looking for but you. They have vanished in an air thick with questions. You give them qualities your current life and actual parents lack, such as an iconic music career, riches, fame, and a grungy hipster vibe. (In contrast, my dad, Abe Reimer, the late, great king of the booksellers, wore Ichthus fish ties at work and brown dress socks to the beach. He carried little packets of Caf-Lib in his pocket and enjoyed listening to gloomy German hymns and—for a little pep— the Chuck Wagon Gang. Abe Reimer was ying to Neil Young's yang.)

When you have no answers to your questions, you create ever-ballooning expectations that can never be met, even if your birth father is Neil Young, Captain Kangaroo, or the crown prince of Genovia. That balloon starts out like a cute red blob floating at a kid's party, but when you puff it up with a lifetime of wonderings, it can grow to be the size of the Goodyear Blimp. And we all know that bloater's not coming down to earth gently.

My blimp lost some steam when I found out my first answers about my birth father through the paperwork Dora had filled out before I was born, on file with the Manitoba Post-Adoption Registry. I still didn't know his name, but I knew his height, ethnicity (which wasn't English, as my adoption paperwork indicated), what his parents did for a living, and that for a time he had coached kids in sports.

Sweet molasses! *I* was the spawn of a coach? *My* DNA included a person responsible for inculcating athletic skill into young people? I thought of Mr. O, my jovial junior high gym teacher and coach presiding over my leaden basketball career. He would be more baffled than I at this news. I am many things, but Sporty Spice I am not.

Later on, Dora would tell me his name was Tom. Their brief romance had begun after they met that summer in the city. Dora always felt that Tom had known she was pregnant. She said little to me on the topic, other than she had kept tabs on him and would contact him when the time was right.

Theodora finally called Tom one day at his work.

"It's a girl! She's thirty-one!" Theodora cried joyously into the receiver.

Tom immediately jumped on his desk and joyously began belting out "I Had a Dream." He jumped down and started handing out cigars to his colleagues when the call came through.

Yeah.

Way off on that.

What happened was this: Dora's heart hammered as she haltingly delivered the news from the summer of 1967. She pretended he had no idea. Tom expressed shock. (Let's give him shock, at least.) He began reciting his ethnic and medical history, followed by a litany of reasons why he couldn't—make that *wouldn't*—have a relationship with me:

"I have teenagers, and they are at an impressionable age."

"There's been too much water under the bridge."

And my personal favorite:

"I wouldn't want to compromise my career path."

Dora, unflattened by these shabby responses, charged ahead. "Tom, Lorilee is a wonderful young woman. She's warm and funny. She's a writer. And she has a beautiful baby boy named Jonah, your grandson! He's about eighteen months old and so cute. You should see her next time she comes to Winnipeg. In fact, I believe she's coming in a couple of months. I can see if she could meet you for coffee . . ."

Tom cut her off midsentence, his crooked arrow hitting the bull's-eye. "No," he said. "No. I can't handle a relationship like this right now. Please don't ever contact me again." There was a click, a dial tone, and later, for me, the sound of a Goodyear Blimp, hissing steam into the blue sky.

The Red-Haired Schoolteacher of Bolingbroke, Nova Scotia

The days between Bertha's death and Walter Shirley's own would have been filled with worry. There was no such thing as life insurance, and Walter's family and his in-laws were all dead.

Infected already, Walter would have noticed the dreaded red spots developing on his chest. The fever and nervous delirium would claim him soon. Though Maud doesn't tell us this, I imagine him in that meek yellow house looking down in despair at the sleeping girl in his arms, noting again that she had his own acutely red hair. He might have offered a prayer. Where would Anne end up? Would she ever belong to anyone again?

Blessedly, for Walter, there was little time to agonize.

The tall, thin lady said it all: "Pore creetures, they didn't live much longer; but they was awful happy while they was alive and I s'pose that counts for a good deal."[7]

That good lady eloquently summarized the legacy left by Anne's parents, a birthright Anne discovered further in the faded, yellow letters between Walter and Bertha. In those wrinkled pages Anne inherited a glorious history. The dearest of all was the last letter, which shared in tender detail baby updates to the only person in the world who cared as much as Bertha did.

> *"This has been the most beautiful day of my life," Anne said to Phil that night. "I've found my father and mother. Those letters have made them real to me. I'm not an orphan any longer. I feel as if I had opened a book and found the roses of yesterday, sweet and beloved, between its leaves."*[8]

Anne's native story had been broken in pieces when she bravely knocked on the door of the yellow house, but now those pieces were somewhat bonded together. A new measure of wholeness and peace was hers. She loved the siblings Cuthbert, her real parents in all ways; but like every orphan, her first family members were tucked inside her spirit.

Unlike the mart worker, the jack-of-all-trades, and Sporty Old Spice yammering on about his career, the Walter Shirley unearthed in Anne's visit was a man who would have stayed devotedly Anne's, if he could have, if typhoid had not blotted out his existence.

Maud, with her orphan's heart, knew there was a big difference between *could* and *would*. So she sent Anne on a quest to find a father who would not disappoint her, and we as readers follow eagerly. Because when Anne found Walter Shirley in that consecrated packet of letters, he turned out to be exactly the person she hoped he would be.

· 14 ·

Dear Tom

Risk anything! Care no more for the opinions of others. . . . Do the
hardest thing on earth for you. Act for yourself. Face the truth.

KATHERINE MANSFIELD,
JOURNAL OF KATHERINE MANSFIELD

A FEW SUMMERS AGO, my wonderings about the man whose family data
was bundled in my bones came to a head, and I reached out to him in
a letter. Though I had known Tom's name and address for fourteen
years, I had never tried contacting him before. I had good reasons. For
one thing, showing up at Tom's door seemed like a bad episode of a
daytime talk show. And if I mailed a letter, what if his wife, presumably
in the dark about me, should open it?

More important, I felt fiercely loyal to my dad. It felt unfaithful, fickle
somehow, to dig up facts about my original father. Then when cancer
took Abe before he turned seventy, I realized that time was short. I also
realized that he would always be my dad, the one I'd think of whenever
something really good happened in my life, or something really bad;
the man I'd immediately picture whenever hearing Southern Gospel
music or the German language, or whenever I'd visit a Christian bookstore. He was one of the voices I'd long to hear after someone broke my
kids' hearts—or my own. Loyalty to my dad was probably why I resisted
reaching out to Tom until years after Abe had died.

Besides, in the end, I felt something like a divine hand, nudging me forward.

It started with a burden on my spirit about eight months before. I knew I had to pray for my birth father. I Googled him for the first time in years and discovered my birth grandmother's obituary. I learned that she was a sweet, sassy pioneer girl and a devout Christian, too. The obit also identified Tom's children, my biological half siblings.

It took me all of four seconds to look them up. There's not much resemblance with me. My sister looks nothing like me. In fact, in her Facebook pictures she has friends who look a lot more like me than she does. But one of my brothers? He doesn't look like me either, but he does resemble Jonah so much it's unsettling.

Paternity confirmed! Tom was my birth father. He was getting older and had no grandchildren besides my three kids. Life is short, and I wanted to be the kind of person to choose love. God assured me He would take care of whether Tom's wife intercepted the letter I had written.

August 1, 2013

Dear Tom,

I've been thinking and praying for a while about whether or not I should reach out to you. Obviously, I decided to take the plunge. Life is short, and I want to be the kind of person who chooses love and connection, regardless of the risk.

Our story started forty-five years ago, when you and my birth mother, Theodora Rudineska, had a brief romance. I was

*the result. I want you to know I'm not reaching out in anger or
shame. I'm glad you and Dora broke up and that I was adopted.
I'm so glad God led me to the parents and family He led me to.*

*But lately, I have come to realize that though we may never
meet, you are a part of me, and I am a part of you. I look like
Dora—a lot—but our personalities are not alike. I understand
you are very athletic, while my basketball and volleyball careers in
school were lackluster at best. Still, half of my DNA is yours, and I
think that influenced and shaped me more than I have thought.*

*Let me also say that I am not looking for a father at this late
stage. I had a dad who rocked me to sleep when I was a baby,
drove me and my friends to the mall in Winnipeg blizzards,
and sacrificed everything on a bookseller's salary to send me to
private school and college, and put braces on my teeth. He was
a loving dad and proud opa. My son Jonah's middle name is
Abram, after my dad. He died seven years ago, of lung cancer at
the age of sixty-eight. He never smoked, other than a rhubarb
leaf when he was a kid. And yet, lung cancer took him from us.*

*So I'm not looking for you to fill shoes that are impossible to
fill at this stage. I guess I want the chance to be friends, to learn
more about you and to have you learn more about me and my
incredible family. This may be too much to ask, or it may be
not enough. But something tells me you might be ready, after all
these years, for another chance to connect.*

*I live in Grand Rapids, Michigan, now, and have for twenty
years. I met my husband of twenty-one years at a private
Christian college in downtown Chicago (one of the places that
feels like home to me). Doyle is from Muskegon, MI, an hour
away from here, on Lake Michigan. He's a huge fisherman and
hunter and is the country boy to my city girl. We both love the*

big lake though. I transferred my love for Lake Winnipeg to Lake Michigan: I love not being able to see the other side.

We have three children: Jonah, fifteen; Ezra, twelve; and Phoebe, eight. Jonah is going to get his driver's permit tomorrow! I can't believe it. He's a good kid, a good student who lives to play hockey and lacrosse, fish, hunt, and play guitar. He's played hockey for eight years and now plays for his JV team at Grand Rapids Christian High School, one of the top high schools in Michigan. This season, he got pulled up to play varsity lacrosse even though he was just a freshman (grade 9).

Our Ez is just the sweetest boy, a gifted writer and artist, gymnast and hurdler (this year, he went out for sixth-grade track and shocked himself when he placed third in hurdles and high jump in a five-school meet).

(Any artistic talent on your side? I am artistically inclined, and a pretty decent drawer, but Ezra is truly outstanding. Neither Doyle's parents nor Dora have laid claim yet.) Phoebe is a spark plug, a turbocharged soccer player who loves dogs and friends. She was adopted from South Korea as a baby.

They are my heart and soul.

How do I not make this sound like a Christmas letter? This is so hard to write.

I grew up in North Kildonan, like all good Mennonite children. My dad immigrated to Canada at age ten from Germany via Ukraine, and my mum grew up in McTavish, Manitoba, near Rosenort and Morris. I have one brother, Dan, who is two and a half years younger than I am. He was also adopted, and we grew up knowing that we were loved.

We were well loved by our parents, grandparents, and huge extended families, especially our Loewen family in Rosenort.

I believe I have forty-four first cousins! Crazy, and fun. My dad was a bookseller, and my mum was a nurse (but only after I turned fifteen and she went back to work). Highlights of my childhood were trips to Woodstock, Ontario, and Fernie, BC, to visit cousins, weeks at Camp Arnes, and days at Grand Beach and Rushing River. In the winter, I remember tobogganing, snowmobiling with my cousins at the floodway, and 7-Eleven nosebleed tickets to see the Jets. I still love the Jets with a burning passion that draws admiration and ire from fans here of the Red Wings. I cried when they were abducted to the desert by Bettman, and I cried when they came back home!

My major in college was broadcasting. I knew I wanted to be a journalist, and I dreamed of being the next Jane Pauley. Pretty quickly I realized broadcasting was not for me. It was way too techie—all those input/output plugs and wires! I can hardly replace batteries in my camera.

Writing was always my first love, and I've been lucky enough to be the author of twelve books.

Doyle and I got married in 1991. He's a wonderful guy, a computer programmer who would rather be a fishing guide. We are close to his family and grateful they live so close.

My last book of twelve is called My Journey to Heaven, *and I wrote it collaboratively with a darling seventy-seven-year-old man who had a heaven experience. I had been cynical about those experiences, but meeting Marv convinced me wholly (within about a minute) that his trip to the other side had been bona fide. Marv, who died about eight months before the book came out, became a bonus dad to me. I am so grateful.*

Yes, a "bonus dad." In my life I've had a few dear people who have been fathers and mothers to me and my kids. Grandpa

George is one example. He and his wife, Grandma Pat, came into our lives through their daughter, Rachel, a friend of mine in college. We reconnected when Doyle and I moved to Grand Rapids. Rachel became a missionary and moved overseas, and so they started inviting Doyle and me over for home-cooked meals, even though Rachel was gone. When I was in a terrible car accident in 1997, Pat came and nursed me at home for two weeks. After that, they were stuck with us forever, and they readily agreed to be a special grandma and grandpa to our kids when they came soon after.

(Jonah just came upstairs to tell me Grandpa had stopped by with one hundred dollars for him to spend on his mission trip to Pittsburgh, for which he leaves tomorrow. Tears welled up as I reflected again that they could not love my kids more if they were their blood relatives.)

Which brings me to this thought: I very much hope you will consider opening your heart to me, to us, and consider it a "bonus" in your life and in the lives of your family. I am guessing my existence is a secret that you have not shared with many people, and that sharing it is an overwhelming, maybe terrifying thought. In my experience, secrets hold you hostage, while the truth, though painful and scary, leads to peace. I understand you are from another generation, one that doesn't share secrets easily, and that it could be extremely difficult for you to tell the people you love that you have a child out there, and grandchildren, too. I'm guessing this news would be hardest to share with your wife, who has no biological connection to me at all.

If it helps, I have a very nice relationship with Bill, Dora's husband. He was an only child, and they only had one child, Danica, so they have a small family. He said something so beautiful, years ago, when Dora and I reconnected and he had a chance to process it all (she had kept my birth a secret for thirty years). He said that he didn't have a lot of family members and that he was happy to welcome a few more, especially since he liked me and Doyle so well. He's a favorite person of ours, by the way, and he's not "related" to us either!

I've taken a month to write this letter, now a mini-nonfiction book. I've had to lay it down often because of other deadlines, because it's summertime and the kids are only little once, and because it's just so loaded. What do I tell you? How will you receive it all? Do you even care? I just simply don't know. And if I never finish it, I never have to send it . . .

I do know that, according to Dora, you were told about my existence about fourteen or fifteen years ago (but you might have already known). You had said "no" then to a relationship with me, and some other things that were pretty hard to hear. (Your career path? Really?) I know you may not have said it all exactly as Dora interpreted it. Maybe you just didn't know what to say.

I'm glad I heard about your "no" when my life was stable and grounded in faith and family. I was terribly hurt for a time and angry that you weren't even willing to meet me for coffee to tell me about your side of the family. I thought you owed that to me, and I still think so. But, all things considered, I got over it. I felt it was your loss in many ways, and I was able to look at the situation objectively. You weren't rejecting me and my beautiful baby (now a beautiful teenager with a driver's permit), because you didn't even know us. I forgave you a long time ago and have prayed for you many times over the years.

I've known your name since then, so of course I looked you up in the phone book immediately, but I have always respected *your privacy. Besides, showing up at your door is not my style and seems like a bad episode of a cheesy talk show . . .*

In February, I looked you up and found your mother's obituary. She sounds like she was an extraordinary lady, which thrilled me. I love her name, and that she was a strong woman of faith. I read the obituary over the phone to my mum, who said, "She sounds just like you!" I know she is among that great cloud of witnesses now, praying for you, and now me, too.

I should wrap this up.

I've given you lots to think about.

I've been resistant all these years to writing, because I was worried that it would be read first by someone who didn't know about me. I did not want to cause drama for you, so I never wrote. But like I said, the last six months have been different. I have felt led to reach out and leave the matter of your wife possibly reading this in hands stronger than mine. I know those strong hands are working in both your lives to prepare you for this letter.

What if you never actually did shut the door on a relationship? What if you did at the time, but have come to think differently and maybe regret it? What if you are ready now?

I hope you let that old secret out in the light of day, but I won't pressure you. I want healing and happiness in this for you, too. But please do let me know if you got my letter so the suspense does not kill me outright.

With a hope and a prayer,

Lorilee

· 15 ·

(He Did Not Say Dear) Lorilee

Though my father and mother forsake me, the LORD will receive me.

PSALM 27:10, NIV

TOM'S WIFE DID NOT INTERCEPT MY LETTER. He got to the mail first that day. And within a week, he sent me a long letter in response.

When I saw the envelope, I knew the timing would be either fantastic or atrocious, depending on what I would find inside. Just a week beforehand, I had been blindsided, let go from my beloved job as an entertainment writer at the *Grand Rapids Press* after seventeen and a half years. "Corporate consolidation" was the reason given, and I was in full sackcloth and ashes over it. That job had been my dream come true, the making of me. Now it was over, and I was completely bereft, grieving the loss of income, work camaraderie, and mostly my identity as an entertainment writer, which was forged in countless rock, pop, and country concerts, provocative plays, frothy musicals, interviews, and backstage encounters. I was the girl who interviewed rock stars and actors, who had a humdinger of a story to tell at any given time about, say, an eighties heavy metal singer falling asleep three times during our interview, or (my favorite) Henry Winkler, aka The Fonz, a kindred spirit, kissing me twice and making Doyle feel a bit like Potsie Weber.

I went to all the shows for free and formed real, sacred friendships with a few entertainers, including (my favorite) James "JY" Young of the band Styx. This is who I *was*, a journalist who bore witness to the pop culture conversation in our city and beyond—a person with my (nonfavorite) photo in the paper, someone recognized out and about and approached constantly for my opinion about who would be kicked off *Dancing with the Stars* and other grave matters of public discourse. I knew in my mind I had been let go for legitimate business reasons, but my orphan's heart felt like it had been hit by a sledgehammer. Once again, the cracks were pinging: *See, you're not good enough*; *obviously, you are not worthy of your dream job*; and *now you go back to being a nobody.*

And now here in my hands was another potential grenade. The ground underneath me felt shaky and soft. Would this letter raise my spirits or be another two-by-four to the psyche?

I thought the fatness of the sealed envelope boded well. Here was the first sign of acknowledgment, and I had waited forty-five years to receive these words. He had held this paper. I ran my fingers over the neatly handwritten address. He had formed each word.

After decades of not getting even a dial tone, someone was picking up the line.

I ripped open the letter:

(He Did Not Begin with Dear)

Lorilee,

I have decided to compose a reply to your recently received letter. I do know that many adopted children actively seek their biological parents; others seemingly don't have any interest.

Firstly, my long ago, very short relationship with Dora . . .

Tom describes his relationship with my birth mother as "four or five encounters" that took place between late May and late June 1967, which, "whereby, using a nine-month calculation" made himself a "probability" to be my birth father.

I will now endeavor to present a brief history of myself, including ancestry, ethnicity, and any pertinent health issues . . .

I will now endeavor to cry my eyes out, I thought. Tom continued on with his CV. The letter, which devoted a full page and a half to health, sounded like an application for a life insurance policy. He gave me his precise ethnic makeup—even his life philosophy:

I am now [a] pretty hard-core secular humanist.

And finally:

Lorilee, you are obviously a wonderful person, BUT I have come to a conclusion that I am unable to deal with and cannot handle an ongoing relationship of this nature at this stage of my life.

I began to breathe through my mouth, and a curiously painful sensation droned in my chest. Could my birth father really be this indifferent?

If I may be so bold, I would suggest that you already have an idyllic life . . .

No, you may not be so bold, sir. You may not! Tom wrapped up his letter, after nine hundred words coated in ice, to tell me to e-mail him only "if you feel the need to contact me further." Also, he had made the decision not to "broach" this "situation" with his family, as if I was a situation, to be broached or not.

Maybe the worst part? Tom signed off with just his name. Not even a "sincerely yours," as he might sign off on a business letter to his realtor. He didn't have to say "love," although I was hoping for it. I knew that I had harbored that hope by the hairline crack that fissured my heart. He didn't have to say "blessings" or "sweet blessings" or "sweet banana pepper blessings," but he could have said more than what he did. He could have, but all he said was . . .

Tom Gordon

I cried for three days, the kind of helpless tears that fall out when somebody dies. I didn't know I cared this much.

His words were as cool as my letter to him was warm, as walled-off as mine was invitational, as soulless as mine was soulful. I was furious on Dora's behalf, and mine. How dare he be seventy years old and still behave as if none of this—my entire life!—was his responsibility! I felt that he had used a vulnerable young woman, impregnated her, and then *run* from her, from us.

It enraged me that he didn't even mention the *existence* of my children.

I didn't need another dad, but I wanted this missing person to be found, to show up and walk toward me, not away from me. After forty-five years, I wanted him to say something perfect, something like *I have missed you so*, something like *I'm here now, I promise. This time, I will keep you.* It was a strange loss of something I had never experienced, a withholding of a blessing, a connection that had always been possible but never realized.

Doyle read the letter and shook his head. His blue eyes looked concerned. "He just can't handle this."

My friend Sheri came over bearing sugared-up lattes and expertise. "He seems very intelligent," she started off, on the positive. "He seems to be saying two things: that none of it is his fault and that you would be better off without him."

"But why," I railed, "couldn't he even mention my kids? He seems to make no connection whatsoever between them being his grandchildren!"

"He just can't handle that," she said, echoing Doyle. "If he thought about them, it would be too much."

The Guild loaded me onto a stretcher and carried me for days, covering me with love and sputtering indignation.

Troy, whose birth father saga is actually worse than mine, said sometimes people get harder and more unfeeling as they get older, contrary to what we wish.

Becky, feeler and caregiver extraordinaire, sent me this note after I burbled at her on a phone call to New Jersey:

If I was your birth father, I would be the proudest. I would have been on a plane and buying a house on your street. You are worthy of his love. (You have that from the Father who builds His home inside you.) I thought of you today. I was the first car at a just-turned green light. A man, paralyzed and in an electric wheelchair, rolled out in front of me. I waited, of course. The cars, four, five, six deep behind me, honked in fury and impatience. They had no idea. Somehow, I thought of you and your job and now this. How we can't see what's ahead. How we react to what we think is (or isn't) happening. So . . . interpret as you see fit. A time to stop honking and trust great protection is the plan? Are there bigger things on the next block? Slowing down to prepare for saving a life? I mean, who knows. All I know is I experienced it, and all I could think of was you.

A message like this from a kindred spirit can be what it takes to turn the corner. Becky was right. We don't always know why bad things happen, why one day we are tooling along, doing what we think is an ace job at work and life, and then everything falls apart on a dime—or at least it feels like a dime. Like the cars behind her in traffic—furious, honking, impatient—I was devastated by both the loss of my newspaper job and by Tom's rejection, and it was good for me to experience all the anger and grief I needed to experience. It was part of the healing process. But for whatever reason, Becky's message was a green arrow to turn left to the new normal. I was still sore and bruised for a long time, but in terms of Tom, I stopped honking. I saw a vision of my flesh-and-blood father as limited, disempowered, closed-off emotionally and spiritually. He could no sooner respond to me as a true father than a paralyzed man could suddenly get up and walk.

He didn't want to keep me, then or now. My hopes for a relationship with my first father were in cinders. Yet it was clear where I should go with my crashed expectations: to the Father who sent His Son from on high to make His home on my planet, my street, my soul. Unlike my birth father, He's not running from me; He's been reaching for me since time began. Not only can my heavenly Father "handle" me; He carved my name in His hands.[1] He *always* calls me "Dear Lorilee"; He's wanted to call my name since He crafted the stars, calling them each by name. He claims me forever and will keep me forever.

God the Father knew Tom's rejection would hurt me but also

that the temporary pain would give way to healing, clarity, and a new vision. One redemptive piece of it is that now I can be consciously guiding Phoebe as she connects her own birth-father "dots." It's probable she will never meet or even have the chance to exchange letters with Jin. But I get to point her to the Father who never disappears, who never forsakes. I get to bear witness to my own story; yes, it felt wretched to be disclaimed by Tom, again, but I was not left on life's curb, bereft, left behind, and left.

Oh no, that wasn't the finale of my story, because the Divine Author always has a plot twist up His sleeve. He would pick me up, dust me off, bind up my wounds, and lead me away from the ashes of the smoking blimp. He would say, "Hey, kid, hop in this air balloon, and let Me show you things you've never seen so clearly before." He would show me that I did have a Father who was with me—wanting, choosing, and keeping me then, now, and always.

He showed me that, yes, my beginnings had been a complete mess, but that there was no messy "situation" too complicated—no trouble too deep—for Him to reach into through adoption.

God also incited my compassion for the man who was supposed to love me but did not. As if there were a chafing dish at the bottom of my soul, my furious heart started to warm and thaw toward Tom.

I don't know if I will ever have any contact with Tom again, but he's a part of me, slipped in my spirit and my blood. He's in my prayers, along with Dora, Moon, and Jin.

Tom had let me go. And after our brief exchange of letters, I knew he was standing behind that decision. But my real Father found me long ago. And from this, I feel joy, because I will have Him as my Father for all time.

· 16 ·

Twenty Pounds of Brown Sugar
and a Garden Rake

Well now, I'd rather have you than a dozen boys, Anne.
MATTHEW CUTHBERT, IN *ANNE OF GREEN GABLES*

I WASN'T LOOKING FOR MY MATTHEW CUTHBERT the day I traveled along snowy roads to hear a stranger give his eyewitness account of heaven.

To be honest, I didn't think much would come of the night; I wasn't a big fan of "heaven books" to begin with. But a former colleague of mine from a publishing house had asked me to come hear this elderly man's story, to see if maybe there was a book in it somewhere. I went, merely because I try to walk through open doors when I can, and this one seemed to be opening the littlest bit.

There was something about Marv from the start. I sat with about one hundred other folks in the church that day; they were curious about heaven for their own reasons. Some of them had experienced the earth-cracking loss of loved ones; others were dying or their family members were. In a soft voice, Marv retold his experience of leaving his body and flying to heaven for a twenty-to-thirty-minute preview of glory. He spoke of the angels who grabbed one arm each and winged him into the bluest skies, where he saw colors like he had never seen on earth, in swirls of cotton candy and bursts of fireworks.

Somehow the outrageous things this man was saying rang commendable and true. And I found myself believing him more with every sequence of his celestial story. To say I fell under Marv's spell would be to suggest he was casting one. And Marv Besteman, salt-of-the-earth, wholesome, Dutch, banker, golfer, grandpa, was not a spell caster, but a truth teller.

If you'd met him even once, you'd know he was true. You'd know he'd no sooner manipulate the truth about his heaven visit than he would don a tutu and dance down the streets of Sparta, the town where he had been president of the local bank at the time of his retirement. There was no magic, no smoke and mirrors to him or his story, but you couldn't help but be enchanted by Marv. I couldn't, anyway.

He was tall, fit for his age, sported white hair, and had laughter behind his eyes. The first time we met, we shook hands and cracked up about something—the Red Wings versus the Jets, probably. He loved to razz me about hockey. ("Oh, it'll be a *slaughter*," he'd mutter under his breath, when I mentioned the upcoming Jets-Wings game. "There will be *blood* all over the *ice*...")

I decided to take a chance on him and his heaven story, just as he'd taken a chance on me. He hired me to write a book proposal for him, and I started coming over to his condo, where he lived with his wife, Ruth. I'd listen and take notes as his story unwrapped week after week. Their home was warm and sweet, filled with family photos and homemade pillows and crafts. Normally, Ruth would offer me a cup of coffee and a peanut cookie—Marv's favorite. Then he and I would get down to business for about an hour, because that's all Marv could handle at one time. Recounting his story, especially seeing loved ones on the other side, made him very emotional. We ended up with a book deal, and I was thrilled, because by then I was deeply invested in Marv's story and wanted to get the chance to tell it. It also gave us lots of time to hang out, which was the best part of all.

I started to look forward most to the moment when I crossed the threshold of the house and entered the kitchen, where Marv would be waiting to greet me. His eyes would light up. "There's my third daughter," he would say, grinning. Or "There's my kid." Or "There's my sweet girl." Or "Hello, pretty lady." My favorite greeting: "Here's the other woman in my life; come for a peanut cookie, I suppose."

He trusted me to tell his sacred story, a story that God had to kick him in his stubborn Hollander pants to tell, and this was a profound honor. Not only did Marv trust me, but he noticed my gifts and believed in them in a wholehearted way, praising me to everyone from his wife to the guy who came and fixed their thermostat one day.

At least two or three times I messed up the hour when we would be meeting (chalk it up to being featherbrained), but Marv quickly forgave me each time and pretended it didn't matter, even though it did. He raved over the book as a whole and many of its pieces specifically. "You were meant to write my story—only you," he said.

Marv showed me that the angels were closer than I knew, giving me a travelogue and a preview to the land where joy will never end. When it was all over—the book was done and Marv's life was ebbing away—I realized what his biggest gifts to me had been: love with no conditions and devotion with no qualifiers. In this hard, disapproving world, here was a person who approved of me with his whole heart. Here was my Matthew Cuthbert—a kindred spirit, a father, a friend who overlooked my broken fences and saw only flowers.

Someone asked me why my own dad was not my Matthew Cuthbert, which got me to thinking. I loved my own dad dearly; he was and is forever my realest of real dads. But a real dad raises you to be responsible, capable, independent, and sovereign in your own grown-up life. It's up to him to bust your chops when you don't take out the garbage, when you've cheated on a math test, or when you've mown the lawn somewhat carelessly. He doesn't usually have the luxury of overlooking your broken fences because it's his job to make you fix them so you don't live in his basement until the Lord comes back.

Matthew, you'll notice, allowed Marilla to do *all* the heavy lifting in the parenting of young Anne. If there was busting of chops to be done—and whoa Nelly! was there *ever*—it fell to Marilla to bust away.

Normally, not always, but normally, a mom and dad share busting duties, so categorical adoration is usually not an option. But when you're lucky enough, like Anne, me, and Phoebe, to find a Matthew Cuthbert in your life, his love changes you for all time.

On that sacred January day when the ground was petrified with ice and Marv's departure from this earth was precious in the sight of the Lord, I cried in Doyle's arms.

On a day like that, when you know what you have lost, life is diminished, true, but also magnified with thanks. How lucky I was to be loved like that, for just a little while.

When someone loves you like Matthew Cuthbert, you can't help but bloom, unfold, increase, and gain color in your face and your days. When someone looks at you through those eyes, there's nothing you can't do.

···

One of the things I love about Matthew—taken from a long list— is the way he *noticed* Anne; her well-being was at the center of his heart. In the vignette in which Matthew watched Anne and her friends go through lines from "The Fairy Queen," the old farmer noticed a scarcity in the life of the one he adored. It finally dawned on him: Anne, though she sparkled like Orion, appeared drab and colorless next to her friends, all adorned in red, blue, pink, and white. Why must his sister, Marilla, keep her "so plainly and soberly gowned"?[1] A girl who shone like Anne should not be gowned so.

"Christmas was only a fortnight off,"[2] and Matthew Cuthbert decided to act on Anne's behalf and buy her something that would make her feel as beautiful as she was. A new dress with the puffiest of sleeves was just the thing. (By the way, isn't the word *fortnight* delicious? Why have we in North America watered it down to "two weeks"?)

But he would have to sacrifice his comfort to make provision for it, and therein lay the rub.

Two problems stood in his way: (1) Matthew was terrified of women in general and would have strongly preferred not to deal with any female at the counter of a store, and (2) in 1879, one could not buy a ready-made dress, no matter how intimidated one was by strange women. He would not be able to grab a frock and plunk it down without comment as he would a bag of hay seed. No, Matthew Cuthbert, potato farmer, bachelor, pipe smoker, father, would have to *speak* and tell a strange woman exactly what he wanted. This worried the dilly out of him.

But Anne was worth overcoming his fears, or dying in the attempt. It was that simple. In the end, Matthew plotted to go to a store with a surefire *man* behind the counter, so he was quite unstrung when a female salesclerk with "big, rolling brown eyes, and a most extensive and bewildering smile"[3] offered to wait on him. (Could Marie Osmond have been time traveling? Also, why were this lady's eyes "rolling"? Was she unwell?)

Adding to Matthew's distress, the clerk wore a stack of bangles that "glittered and rattled and tinkled with every movement of her hands."[4] His wits were wrecked by the ordeal.

Though "Marie" did nothing outside the bounds of her job and good taste—she did not, say, lunge across the counter and begin chewing on his arm—her femininity and bangles conspired to tie Matthew's tongue to where he could not ask for something so crazy, freaky, scary as a dress—even for Anne. So he asked for several things he didn't need at all and came home with a garden rake and twenty pounds of brown sugar. (This confused Marilla thoroughly, although on the bright side, this would keep them all in black fruitcake and porridge topping until the sun should burn out in the sky.)

Love like Matthew's does not give up easily, however. He engaged a willing Mrs. Rachel to sew this dress, asking only that it be made "in the new way."[5] He hadn't gone a million miles outside his comfort zone only to present another drab dress to Anne. This dress should adorn and make her gleam like the opal-tinted horizon she had once described to him in that dreamy way of hers.

"Puffs? Of course," was Mrs. Rachel's reply.[6] She was on the job, and Matthew needn't worry a speck more about it. That good lady procured some silky brown gloria (a glossy silk and cotton or silk and wool, used in dresses and umbrella coverings) from the general store and went about spinning a gown so shirred, ruffled, pin-tucked, and puffed it would exceed Anne's golden dreams. As she spun this wonder, Mrs. Rachel marveled at the fact that Matthew noticed Anne's drab clothing at all. To think—"That man is waking up after being asleep for over sixty years."[7] But we're not surprised. Matthew Cuthbert was born to be a father.

They say a new father's brain chemistry, like a new mother's, changes when a baby is born. Some primal alchemy in Matthew started to alter from the moment he met Anne. At this point in the story, two-plus years after adopting her, Matthew, once half-awake, was moved and inspired by love in his life. No one saw this change coming, least of all himself. But we are not surprised: Matthew Cuthbert was born to love.

Whenever I read the story of that Christmas morning and the dress reveal, I get a little giddy thinking of Anne, about to receive the gift of her dreams. Sure, the puffs caused some commotion at Green Gables: Marilla called them "ridiculous." How could anyone, she demanded to know, even fit through a doorway with those sleeves?[8]

(I tend to agree with Marilla that those sleeves are *nutty puffy*. In replica frocks, the sleeves appear as if a good gust of wind might blow the wearer clear to Nova Scotia. But on the bright side, Anne would not be in any danger of being submerged in water.)

We watch for the look on Anne's face, and we know it's worth all accusations of wastefulness. Her face was filled with awe; her eyes welled with tears, and not just because she now had the pretty, stylish dress she had longed for. Another dream had come true, the same dream fulfilled whenever a giver connects a gift with his recipient like a bat and a ball.

Gift giving is undervalued, but a present well given can be an oracle of love. It says, *I am crazy about you. I know you. I understand you.* We all dream of being known and understood. And if our hearts are long starved like Anne's was, a gift like this is a feast.

For me, some of the most humble gifts stand the tallest. One long-ago Christmas when I had come home to Winnipeg from college in Chicago, my dad laid a boxed VHS set of the *Anne of Green Gables* movies under the tree. Though they are now obsolete, I will keep them forever. Just try to take those tapes from me. You'd have to rip them out of my cold, dead hands first. Dad also gave me a pink,

Anne-themed address book. I used it to tatters, and it still sits nestled in a basket of treasures.

My mum gave me the other gift just a few years ago. It was a framed photo of Debbie, the polar bear I used to love to visit at the zoo in Winnipeg. Debbie sits behind me in my office, high atop a tall antique dresser. Sometimes when I'm a little lost or stuck, I swivel around and make eye contact with her. *Boy, those were the days, huh? You and me at the zoo, stale popcorn and that zoo-y smell of rocks and grass and algae and wet fur and polar bear pies....* More often than you might think, that link with my past is enough to blow the dust off my present. I'm found again, unstuck and back to work. *I am crazy about you. I know you. I understand you.* These gifts remind me that those things were and are true, even across the curtain that separates earth from heaven.

And then there are the countless gifts from Phoebe's own Matthew Cuthbert, Grandpa George. He isn't related to any of us through blood, marriage, or adoption, but he is our dad and our grandpa in every way that counts. When Doyle and I moved to Grand Rapids twenty-one years ago, he and Grandma Pat tucked us under their wing, and we've remained there ever since. We have so many stories of Grandpa's care for us, but here's a real chestnut: Last year Grandpa spent January 2 with me at a *laundromat,* carrying in groaning loads of asbestos-spewed towels and blankets from the van and feeding quarters into machines.

Let me back up a mite.... At the stroke of midnight on New Year's Day, our old, clanging water pipes burst wide open, and out gushed hot, nasty water all over our clean and dirty laundry. The cats got agitated and peed over the whole thing, and Doyle uncharacteristically got the flu. (This time, he *really* was sick, unlike that one Valentine's Day when I had to review a Barry Manilow concert for the *Press.*)

While we waited for the asbestos removal people to come remove the junk, someone had to deal with that mountain of dirty, wet laundry. Doyle was lying on the couch, moaning, and so it fell to me and wonderful Grandpa. I will never forget the gratitude that welled up in me that day for this modest man, who may be overlooked by some, but to us is a knight and a chief. I was not alone in my time of need, the best offering of all.

Grandpa's gift is showing up, attending every possible musical concert; hockey, soccer, or lacrosse game; track meet; and gymnastics exhibition, sacrificing his comfort in all elements. He is always there for my kids, and they know it, especially Phoebe, who is an apple of his eye. From the time they met, Grandpa could calm her down in a way not even Grandma, a baby whisperer, could do. The two of them have played roughly one hundred games of Sorry and gone for countless ice cream runs in his vintage 1972 white Oldsmobile Cutlass convertible.

Even when Phoebe at age five accidentally jeopardized another of Grandpa's "apples"—somehow taking the clutch out and rolling the convertible backward down their hilled driveway until it hit a stone wall across the street—Grandpa didn't blame her a bit. (By the way, nothing strikes cold, icy dread more efficiently into the heart of a mother than the sight of your daughter and two other small children rolling backward straight into the road.) God preserved us all that day, even the convertible, which sustained a dented fender and a couple of scratches. Really, Grandpa probably blamed himself for not knowing she was strong enough to pull out the clutch, but who could have predicted that? The kid is bionic. She will probably be a human cannonball in the circus when she grows up.

Grandpa George's humble gifts have saved us over and over, and he loves us like his own. We don't deserve him, but somehow he claims us anyway. Like Matthew Cuthbert, and like Jesus, he keeps us—lucky us!—as the apples of his eye, and covers us with his love and protection. We are all changed by a father's good gifts.

...

Anne was a new girl on that Christmas morning, broken on a white, beautiful world. As we read about her gift from Matthew, we are renewed ourselves. Anne became braver as a result, as if love breathed nerve and pluck into her fearful places. Somehow, we too are braver, nervier, less fearful—*puffed up.*

"I knew that I must live up to those sleeves,"[9] she told Diana. She rose to her puffs, and Matthew's faith in her, exceeding her expectations of what she could do. And we gain courage as well, hoping to exceed our Father's high view of us.

Rising above and living well loved, Anne followed every academic rainbow, fueled by the hope of seeing Matthew's kind eyes gleam with pride at her achievement. When Anne discovered she and Gilbert Blythe had tied for first on the island in the Queen's entrance exam, her first thought was to share her joy with Matthew. He was uppermost in her mind, just as she was always uppermost in his.

It's at this point that repeat readers start to get a little sad. We know that dear Matthew will not get the chance to exult in many more of Anne's victories. Oh, there would be her recital performance at the White Sands Hotel and a few more scholarly peaks, but the reaper whose name was death was marching toward Green Gables. On the night Anne once again shared good news with Matthew— that she had won the Avery scholarship—he was thrilled to the gills.

And then he uttered the line that every orphan of every stripe wants to hear: He told her that she was "my girl—my girl that I'm proud of."[10] I imagine his eyes tender and his buttons popping.

This father and daughter didn't know it, but their time together was almost over. "It was the last night before sorrow touched her life; and no life is ever quite the same again when once that cold, sanctifying touch has been laid upon it."[11] When I read Anne for the third time, after my dad's death, I choked up. I, too, had been touched by that hand, and I knew that when you lose someone as essential as a father, your life is never quite the same.

It's hard to believe Matthew and Anne had only four years together. I could start howling right now, couldn't you? Each time I read the story, I know his death is coming—it's not like later editions of the book feature alternate endings—but Matthew's death always breaks me right down to the ground.

So there's the inevitable part where I am predestined to cry, but right before, there's Anne, realizing a truth that will hold her through her grief:

"I'm quite content to be Anne of Green Gables,"[12] she said. She's content to belong, a daughter of simple folk and a meek, small town. No diamonds can compare to the value of pearl beads given to her by Matthew with love.

I can relate.

No *New York Times* chart topper can rival the value of being entrusted to tell Marv's heaven story, to be his "third daughter" for just two and a half years.

No inheritance can compare to being "the Reimer girl from the bookstore," daughter of the late, great craftsman of bookselling. Because of my dad's influence, I write, I read, and I stack teetering piles of books by my bed (and along the wall, for half the length of the room). On account of my dad, who suffered as a child of war and then as a refugee in a new land, I have a lifelong soft spot for outcasts, underdogs, and strangers. I aspire to his humility and kindness for all people. These are my heirlooms, not because of biology, but because one man opened his heart to love another man's child.

Phoebe, who never got the chance to really know her doting opa, has been blessed with her own Matthew Cuthbert. No horse-drawn carriage ride could be more wonderful than cruising in Grandpa's white convertible; no banquet could be more delicious than sharing cookie dough ice cream on a summer's evening.

Anne, Phoebe, and I—we are the lucky ones, loved by fathers who were not obliged by blood to care but did anyway. Above all, Matthew Cuthbert cared. Overlooked all his life by others, Matthew did not speak in the tongues of men or angels—he hardly spoke at all. He was patient and kind. He had no ego. He did not dishonor others, was not self-seeking or easily angered. Though his girl was often in the wrong, Matthew kept no record. He always protected, always trusted, always hoped, and always persevered. His love never failed her.[13]

Matthew Cuthbert reminds me of another adoptive father, one who gives good and perfect gifts and tells each one of us, "You're My girl—My girl I'm proud of."

When Someone loves you like that, you can't help but bloom, unfold, increase, and gain color in your face and in your days. When Someone looks at you through those eyes, there's nothing you can't do.

A Bend in the Road

The world breaks everyone and afterwards many are strong at the broken places.
ERNEST HEMINGWAY, *A FAREWELL TO ARMS*

COMING BACK TO PRINCE EDWARD ISLAND feels like coming home, even though I know better. In the past few years, I've made two more trips to "the land cradled by waves,"[1] and by now I know I will never belong completely. If I bought my dream house—near Cavendish with eggplant-purple shingles, white trim, and a sliver of an ocean view—tomorrow, adopted a PEI brogue, and served its extraordinary potatoes with every meal, I'd still be from "away." Islanders are very particular about that point.

Yet even though I know the island will never be my home, it has taken up permanent residence in my heart. That's why for years I'd been eager to introduce my family to Anne's dreamy ocean home. Once Phoebe was old enough to be able to enjoy such a trip, the time had come. Secretly, though, I was a little worried: Would my guys appreciate it as much as my daughter and I would?

After leaving Grand Rapids, I gave Jonah and Ezra strict orders to visit Green Gables with a good attitude. "We're going to do stuff that you love—there *will* be adventures," I told them. "But on Thursday we are going to Green Gables, and *you are going to like it very, very much.*" Mothers of teenage boys—undoubtedly you've all made similar speeches to your own cherubs.

On a hot Thursday in August, the five of us headed out to Cavendish. We stopped first at the replica of the post office run by Maud's grandparents, assisted by Maud, once upon a time. Ezra tagged along with me as I carefully examined every artifact and read every caption. At one point, I looked around for Jonah and saw that he had passed out from boredom. He was slumped over in a chair in the corner, fast asleep. He would later say he *had* a good attitude but was merely unconscious.

Then we walked over to Green Gables itself. Because we were there at the peak of tourist season, actors dressed up as Anne and Gilbert were greeting pilgrims at the door.

"So what are you doing over here, Gilbert Blythe?" I demanded of the young man sporting a jaunty cap and suspendered pants.

"Oh, you know, we're 'studying,'" he said, making jarringly modern air quotes around the word. Oh Gilbert, you frisky biscuit, you.

A few minutes later, I asked the guide where the red currant wine was. "Diana drank it all," she said.

Jonah snored in the car while patient Ezra and I pored over the writerly details of the LMM homesite. Meanwhile, Phoebe bounced through Green Gables with Doyle, pausing only to admire her very favorite piece of Anne-a-phernalia: the slate!

However un-enthralled Jonah was with that afternoon at Green Gables, he—and all of us—had fallen under the island's spell (although he wouldn't put it in quite so fat and buttery of terms). We found plenty to adore on the island, which holds lots of spectacular adventures for all types, not just mooning middle-aged women chasing the ghost of Gilbert Blythe. We quickly became addicted to the hunt for glittery sea glass treasures scattered on PEI's beaches, one of the world's troves, after Jonah unearthed an elusive sky-blue piece he found.

In the quest for adventure, we spent two glorious days in the company of Captain Perry, a character straight out of a romance novel or an Old Spice commercial, and his young crew, Chanel and Lucais. The first day we fished for mackerel, reeling in the silvery fish hand over fist while taking in the sights of seals and lighthouses. Phoebe and Captain Perry were fast friends, and within an hour she was wearing his hat and driving the boat. The next morning, we boarded Captain Perry's boat again, this time for a clam-digging spree, donning wetsuits and raking a sandbar floor for clams. Once we had combed a potful, we explored a nearby deserted island while the crew barbecued our catch for lunch. On another evening, the five of us clapped our hands and stomped our feet to the raucous Celtic fiddles, bagpipes, and step-dancing at a "kitchen party" or *ceilidh* (Cay-lee). These musical gatherings, which feature Gaelic folk music and dancing, reflect the island's Scottish heritage.

And for one heavenly afternoon, we rented bikes in PEI National Park, formed a line, and cruised along a pristine trail with Atlantic waves and lighthouses on one side and woodlands on the other. We wound our way to the world-famous Dalvey-by-the-Sea hotel, where we sipped iced tea on the same porch as the Duke and Duchess of Cambridge when they relaxed there during their post-wedding Canadian tour. Of course, like a good royal subject, I forced my American children to have their pictures taken next to a cardboard cutout of the future king and queen.

If you ever visit the Island, with or without the cherubs, do not miss the chance to dine on PEI potatoes. What's that, you say? A potato is a potato? *Uh-uh. Nope. Wrong.* These taters elevate the humble spud to something sublime, in whatever form, but mashed is the pinnacle. You'll want to bathe in a vat of them, I promise.

As much as I enjoyed romping around the island with my family, I realized that it is abundantly easier to plunge into Anne minutiae without them. And so, not long after, I began planning my third visit. This time, I invited my friend Kim to come along. A radiant soul, Anne-fan girl, and world traveler, Kim is always up for a caper of some sort—that, and she always manages to find flights at a massive discount. So it would be: PEI, ready or not, here we come!

...

On my third trip, I came specifically to engage with this place, this story, and to get a closer look at Maud and her literary daughter who spoke my own language of being lost and found. She made sure Anne was found and kept, but one reason I'd been drawn back to the island was to find the answer to the question: Was Maud ever found?

I didn't know, as Kim and I drove through November's mists to our inn, that I would stumble upon some insights the next day. Tourist season was over for the year, and everything was closed tight until May. Thankfully, the worthy ladies at PEI Tourism helped us out and arranged for four openings, all on one day.

Our first stop that morning was the post office in Cavendish. We had to be specially let in and supervised by a Canada Post employee (even the post office was shut down for the season). The cozy little building is an ode to the arduous treks of manuscripts at the turn of the twentieth century. One display depicted a piece of mail's journey through horse-drawn sleigh, train, iceboat, and steamer to get to the mainland. I counted myself lucky to be able to press "send" with my query letters and book proposals—no iceboats involved.

Overlooked by most tourists, to me, it's a capstone of understanding Maud as a writer. This is the place where Maud received numerous rejections of her articles and where she had borne the disappointment of even *Anne* being passed over five times. Here at the post office was a display of her at work, stamping and sorting envelopes and parcels. Here she also toiled away at her covert craft, scribbling stories and imagining worlds. As a writer now for twenty-two years, I felt more kinship with Maud with each discovery I made. I understood how lonely the writing life can be—lonely, and for her, clandestine. As I stopped at each display case, I was moved by several quotations from Maud that appeared alongside artifacts. "All of these doings," she said, "were conducted in profound secrecy."[2]

No one was the wiser of her writings or rejections, which was key to Maud trying at all. She would have given up writing completely if the whole town would have been privy to those returned parcels. Thank Providence, then, for her job as a postmistress, and for nudging Maud to give *Anne* a final shot at success. "The manuscript lay in a hatbox until I came across it one winter day while rummaging." Maud's words are enlarged in a display with a picture of her, a postage scale, and a sorting cupboard. "'I'll try once more,' I thought."[3]

I broke out in goose bumps. *I'll try once more....* Every writer can relate to trying and trying, and wondering when it's time to try once more or give it up. It takes so much wisdom to know the difference. I peered at an enlarged photograph of Maud's face. There was humor in her expression, and even her mouth suggested the possibility of it, reflecting what she once wrote about Marilla.[4] I looked in her flickering eyes and felt a rush of approval from my writing godmother. I wanted to step back in time and ask her so many questions. I wanted to sit at her feet and learn from a master.

...

At Green Gables, another official opened the doors for us. We had the run of the place for an hour.

Green Gables.

To ourselves.

For an hour.

Had it not been for gravity, I would have bonked my head on the ceiling. I looked at Kim with glee. We may have squealed. We may have also made snow angels on the kitchen floor. The sweet Parks Canada official giggled and indulged our frolics. Little did she know her presence was the only thing keeping us from licking stuff.

We swooned at the details easily spotted by fans: Marilla's amethyst brooch; Anne's brown gloria with giant puffs, hung on the closet door of her room; and a slim jar of raspberry cordial in the pantry. I took a picture of the cracked slate, knowing Phoebe would ask about it, and fondly remembered the hot summer's day when she'd raced through the house.

Now, in sleeting November, I lingered in the east bedroom, Anne's room, which she had fluffed and feathered into a nest that fed her craving for beauty and comfort. It was a haven now, a place to belong. Here she had been changed from the lost foundling girl, on trial for a home, to Anne of Green Gables and nowhere else. In this room, she transcended the broken road of orphanhood, her feet now bound for a bright future. She consistently chose the path of joy and grace, and that had made all the difference. And here she had dreamed of the bend in the road.

In the last chapter of the first book, we find Anne at a crossroads. Matthew was gone, and Marilla planned to sell the farm and move in with Rachel Lynde. Anne made a tremendous sacrifice, giving up her four-year scholarship to Redmond College to stay home and help Marilla keep Green Gables. She saved the home she loved but at great cost.

Anne again chose the elevated path. She didn't dwell on what she had lost, but rather on what she'd found. "When I left Queen's my future seemed to stretch out before me like a straight road. I thought I could see along it for many a milestone. Now there is a bend in it. I don't know what lies around the bend, but I'm going to believe that the best does."[5]

...

The next stop for Kim and me: the village of Park Corner to visit Silver Bush, the home of Maud's cousins. On the way I spotted a vista, just beyond a bend in the road. It was much too beautiful to fly by. We stopped the car and got out, the bitter wind whipping through our hair. There were blue inlets on both sides of the road, with a cluster of candy-colored fishing huts on the right. The sea just beyond smashed and roared. God's love seemed to stir through me with the wind, and I thanked Him again for bringing me back to this place.

Miraculously, we found an open gas station and pulled up the driveway in search of food. Kim rolled down her window and bellowed at the guy who materialized in the doorway. "We're not from around here!" The man, a crinkly-eyed fisherman type, didn't miss a beat. "Z'at so?" he said. It was obvious to the mussels in the harbor that we were not from around there. The sub sandwiches we bought from him were surprisingly good.

Silver Bush smelled like apples and cinnamon. The proprietor, a double relative of Maud's, had mulled some in a pot on the ancient stove upon our arrival. Where Green Gables felt like a museum, Silver Bush wrapped us up like a home. Indeed, the Scottish Campbells settled in this spot in 1776 and have lived there to this day. Maud loved to return to this wonder castle in her words and stories. Her novels *The Story Girl*, *Pat of Silver Bush*, and *Mistress Pat* are set here.

"Take all the time you need," the current Ms. Campbell said. "Look at whatever you like." We didn't have to be told twice. Once more, Silver Bush seemed inhabited by the people who lived and loved within its four walls. We took our time.

I paused at the mantel where Maud married Reverend Ewan MacDonald when she was thirty-seven, wishing she had instead found her Gilbert, or even that she had taken a chance with Herman. Ewan hid his mental illness from her, and Maud's marriage was dark and turbulent, even nightmarish at times. Ewan's madness grew deeper as he obsessed that he was not one of the elect and therefore predestined to hell. How Maud suffered through his darkness, and her own.

When I looked into the glass panes of the very bookcase into which lonely Maud had stared, I, too, saw the imaginary Katie Maurice staring back at me. I was walking in Maud's footsteps, and she and Anne felt very close by. At Silver Bush, Maud had found a sense of belonging, an orphan no more. I felt sad that she ever had to leave this place, that she hadn't been given a permanent spot at the table. Here she would have been kept ungrudgingly, and what a difference that would have made.

Warming my hands by the stove, I talked it over with Ms. Campbell, whose own mother was adopted as a baby from the Charlottetown orphan asylum. She understood my feelings but pointed out that Maud's loss was not unredeemed. "Had she grown up differently, would she be the person who wrote *Anne of Green Gables*?"

...

We might also wonder whether Maud would have written *Anne of Green Gables* if she'd spent her early life away from her adored Prince

Edward Island. In fact, after her wedding, she moved with her husband to Ontario. Never again would the island be her home.

It bothered me when I learned that Maud, who endured numerous disappointments in her personal life, may have taken her own life in April 1942, via a drug overdose. A note was left by her bed that read, in part, "I have lost my mind by spells and I do not dare think what I may do in those spells."[6] Her granddaughter, Kate Macdonald, came forward with this news in 2008—bravely, I thought—to raise awareness about mental illness. But some scholars and relatives have said they believe that the overdose was accidental.[7]

Only God knows for sure how Lucy Maud Montgomery died, but in some ways, it doesn't matter. She was in agony either way. Her life was full of painful cracks, but I wanted to believe that the light had filtered in. Had there been hope in her darkness?

Unbeknownst to me, I would find an intriguing clue during our final appointment of the day. It was getting dark at four thirty in the afternoon when we circled back to Cavendish to meet with John and Jennie Macneill, who live next door to Green Gables and run the place known formally as the Site of Lucy Maud Montgomery's Cavendish Home.

We could hear the ocean nearby, moaning and churning, talking to us. It was snug and welcoming in the Macneills' lamp-lit farmhouse, which Cousin Maud had visited many times. Once, when John was a little boy, she came for Sunday lunch, although he admits the visit made no great impression on his six-year-old self. His father was Maud's first cousin, but Jennie was the true expert on all things concerning "the author," as she reverently referred to her.

Their first-rate bookstore was closed for the season, but we talked shop anyway, specifically about the splendid new covers that had been released that fall for the Anne and Emily books. The Macneills had opened their bookstore and the homesite in the late 1980s. "When the author's journals came out in 1985, we found out how much she loved this land," Jennie said.

There's nothing left of Maud's childhood home but the stone foundation; nothing, that is, except for the fields and lanes she walked, the gardens she tended, and the old trees she sat under to dream and write. *Anne of Green Gables* was written here, as well as other books. Some people come to the site and are disappointed to see only a hole in the ground where a house used to be. Kindred spirits see much more.

Jennie, eighty-four, got out her fine china and brewed us some Red Rose tea with milk and sugar. It was delicious. We sat at her kitchen table, sipping our tea as she answered my questions about Maud in general and specifically her feeling like an orphan. "I don't think she would have written *Anne* if she had been brought up in a house with other children and activity," Jennie said. "She was brought up by two old people in a quiet house."

In a lull, I could hear the sea tossing nearby. I could've stayed in that kitchen forever.

Jennie leaned in, her blue eyes bright with memory. "Do you know," she said, "I was twelve when I attended the author's funeral?" I couldn't believe my ears. I was drinking tea with an eyewitness. I drew my chair closer.

"My mother was one of the ladies who scrubbed the church in the morning," she said. "Maud wanted to come home and be buried among her kith and kin."

Heads of government, including the premier of Prince Edward Island, and the Presbyterian clergy were present at the funeral. An old minister friend of Maud's, Reverend Sterling, presided as twelve-year-old Jennie sat in a hard pew. He began to retell the third story in *Chronicles of Avonlea*, called "Each in His Own Tongue," as a way to eulogize Maud.

The profound chronicle stands alone in a collection of jolly domestic comedies—a rare, dark red piece of sea glass among breezy blues and greens. Jennie told me that it was her favorite yarn of Maud's whole catalogue.

The story tells of another twelve-year-old, Felix, yet one more orphan, with a soul full of music, the apple of his grandfather's eye. A violin prodigy, Felix longed to play the fiddle like his late father, but his grandfather forbade it, thinking he was preserving the boy for a life in the ministry.

The grandfather, Reverend Leonard, had failed to see that "a man may minister to the needs of humanity in many different but equally effective ways."[8] This fact becomes clear at the deathbed of the town Magdalen, a sinner and a castaway who didn't believe God could forgive her many sins.

The minister assured her, "God will forgive you if you ask Him. . . . He can and He will. He is a God of love, Naomi. . . . God loves us like a father."[9] But her father had loved her badly, as so many fathers do—as Maud's father had, and as Tom and Jin do. To speak of a loving father doesn't always help.

"Jesus Christ forgave and loved the Magdalen. . . . Christ died for you, Naomi," Reverend Leonard added. "He bore your sins in His own body on the cross."[10] Naomi's tortured soul was on the rack, and the truth of his words didn't penetrate her soul. Reverend Leonard could only plead with God. "Help this woman. Speak to her in a tongue which she can understand."[11] That language turned out to be Felix's music, and he played the fiddle as if the melodies were sequences in the Magdalen's life: the innocence of childhood, the anguish of a heart deceived, despair, the casting away of all that's good, then repentance and a plea for pardon. Finally, Felix's music offered a message of redemption, as the fiddle conveyed "great, infinite forgiveness, an all-comprehending love . . . healing for a sick soul . . . light and hope and peace."[12]

Felix laid down his fiddle, and peace that passed understanding crossed the Magdalen's dying face. She understood at last that she was forgiven and loved, and the grandfather comprehended that each must tell his message in his "own appointed way."[13]

Old Reverend Sterling was overcome with emotion as he tried to retell this story at Maud's funeral.

"I sat there and thought, *Goodness, he's making an awful mess of it*," Jennie said, tearing up. "He kinda got lost. I wanted to jump over the pews and help him, in front of the premier and all the dignitaries."

By then, there wasn't a dry eye in the kitchen of the Macneills' farmhouse. We were all sitting in a hard pew with Jennie in 1942, dabbing our eyes. At Maud's funeral, Reverend Sterling had tried to say that Maud had lived her life ministering to the needs of humanity in her own appointed way, which was wondrous and true. But I took more from the story.

I hoped that somewhere, in the pits of Maud's splintered, shadowy heart, she had found healing for a sick soul, light and hope and peace.

Throughout her journals and letters, Maud had been open about her spiritual doubts and questions about Christianity. Yet I had always balanced accounts of her skepticism with stories like "Each in His Own Tongue," which are full of keen awareness of our human failings and our need for redemption. To doubt, after all, is to be human, and Maud had more demons than most, more reasons to question, to fall into hopelessness and despair. The last years of her life were full of turbulence and pain; her final recorded note reads in part, "God forgive me."[14] Had she cried out to her Father at the end—and at last grasped His love for her as His daughter?

When Kim and I visited Maud's grave a little while later, it was dark, and the sea keened like an evil thing, the wind and rain nipping at our faces. But my thoughts were as light as an opal-tinted horizon. *Did you rest in the mercy of the One you gave voice to through the elderly minister and his grandson's violin? Were you, like the Magdalen in your story, held at last by a perfect Father's all-consuming love?*

...

Seventy-three years after Maud's death, her greatest legacy remains Anne, a character to whom she gave everything she herself hoped for in life. Maud's red-headed orphan girl found deep friendship in Diana and later in other bosom pals. She discovered a kindred mate in Gilbert, someone who admired her intellect and ambition. Anne found home, family, and belonging with Matthew and Marilla at Green Gables.

Though Maud didn't want to revisit Anne's story beyond the first book, she did so in large part to pay the bills. In the next seven books, she reveals numerous bends in the road for the girl we first meet at age eleven, clad in a tight, scratchy castaway's dress. Readers follow Anne to college, to her first teaching posts, to her marriage to Gilbert and motherhood to six children—Jem, Walter, Shirley, Nan, Di, and Rilla.

Anne encounters dear, like-minded souls along the way—she begins to call them "the race that knows Joseph"—including several incarnations of Mrs. Rachel, her first foe-then-friend. Our Anne faces profound joy and cavernous sorrows.

Maud even takes Anne by the pen and guides her to the shabby, yellow house, where she realizes that her birth parents, Walter and Shirley, had loved her, a treasure most orphans never find.

Through Anne, Maud speaks volumes about the desire we all have to belong and to matter to the people we love. Countless readers, including me and my girl, have come to understand friendship, abiding love, and the power of redemption in a more significant fashion.

By way of Anne, millions of people from around the world have gained some portion of healing as they recognize the orphan in themselves. We grasp now that however we may be bereft, left behind, and left, there is always the bend in the road. Grace will always meet us there.

...

CERTIFICATE OF ADOPTION

Worm to adopt: Harry Mockabee

New parent: Phoebe Craker

Old parent: Lauren Mockabee

New name: Harry Cracker

Godparents: Doyle Craker and Brooke V.

I will respect my new child and help him survive. — Signed, Phoebe Craker

Presenting "Harry Cracker's" certificate of adoption, otherwise known as, "Whereupon I became the grandmother of a mealworm." It showed up in the flotsam of Phoebe's backpack one day. When pressed, my girl just shrugged and said she and her pally were "playing adoption." At least something good came from the fourth-grade Spanish immersion mealworm unit.

I didn't let on, but I was thrilled. Phoebe doesn't say too much about being adopted, but this showed me she was resolving her first, unremembered loss in her own way. Sometimes she asks when we are going to visit Korea, and I tell her that we'll go when we are able and that I can't wait. Once in a while, she'll suddenly say something about her birth mother. About a year ago, she wrote her a letter and had Ezra draw a picture of her in pigtails.

At the last Olympics, she cheered like a whirling dervish for one country, and it wasn't the USA or Canada. She was looking for her missing people in Korean athletes, seeking her first loves, culture, and language, just as I found meaning in rooting for the True North. We always reach for home.

At times I'll stare at Phoebe, amazed that I got to bring her here to live with me, with us. *Oh wild one, never change. You're going to bring fire and zing to a cold, numb world.*

I remember the first afternoon we brought her back to our hotel room in Seoul. She was stoic at first, unsure of what was happening, but probably hoping that these strangers who looked and smelled and felt weird would return her to her doting foster parents. For four days we did just that: spending time alone with Phoebe for several hours before sending her back to her foster home.

On that Friday evening, however, we did not return her. When she realized she wasn't going back, she began to scream. She screamed all night, or at least it felt like all night. I held her in my arms in the orange baby carrier and paced the floors of our small suite in the adoption agency's hospitality house. Doyle, who almost never needs more sleep than me (my kids call me "Sleeper Deeper"), was out cold, somehow slumbering through his daughter's shrieks.

The only thing that remotely worked as a lulling agent was to stand in front of the bathroom sink and let the water run over Phoebe's tiny feet. Somewhat mollified by the sound or the feel or both, my little Gonju sniffled and gazed at the running water. Sometimes, she and

I would lock eyes in the mirror above the sink, and neither one of us looked away. We were taking the measure of each other. Who would back down first?

I stood fatigued, done in, and heartsick. Yet something in me rose up like a warrior. I would soldier on all night and all day for this frenzied, mottled baby girl. I would take a bullet to the head for her. I would not give up until she knew that she was safe and that I could be trusted.

It's me and you, baby. You will not win this one. This is what moms do; we fight. I will always fight for you, even when you're brawling like a prize fighter, like you are now, no matter what. We belong together now . . .

In the wee hours, she finally fell asleep. Then the early morning calm was broken by her piercing cry as she woke up. She screamed much of the way home on a Korean airline, with Koreans trying to help us but making things worse. I would go to the airplane bathroom and cry my own eyes out. It was not the way I wanted to start out life with my daughter. Yet each time I walked back to my seat, I felt a renewed resolve to battle for her orphan's heart.

Nine years later, though, I still hear those screams. They were the cries of grief, at being ripped from everything she knew: her Appa and Eoma (Mommy and Daddy), foster siblings, her home, heritage, and beginnings. Her heart had broken like a bone.

That break belongs to everyone who has ever been bereft, left behind, and left—in other words, to Maud, to Phoebe, to all of us. But God mends and makes us strong at the broken places.

When she brought home that adopted worm, I vowed again to invest in her heart, to enter into the painful places and encourage understanding, acceptance, and forgiveness.

I need to beg for wisdom and patience like a waterfall, every single day.

Phoebe has to do her own work. I would give my left foot to do it for her. But that's not the way it works. I can't rescue or fix her. She has to discover her own truth and healing. But I can walk close to her and cheer her on, especially if she decides to search for Moon someday.

I can tell her she's worth fighting for. I can tell her that our cracked stories don't have the last word, not by a long shot.

Baby girl, believe that the best things lie around the bend in the road. Stay fascinated with the road beyond! Speak in your own tongue and minister to the needs of humanity. Never forget.

I can tell her that our heart-bones are healing because we belong to Jehovah Rapha.

He said that there could be a better way; that all things could be made new.

Everyone wants to feel secure and wanted. We all want to belong.

He said He would not leave us as waifs on the street; He comes for us. He never forgets the children whose names are written in the palm of His hand. God makes us belong. He is enough.

At every bend in the road, our Father is waiting for us, reaching out His arms. And we are orphans no more.

Acknowledgments

Where to start? So many kind folks were a great help to me in writing this book—soooo many.

Thank you, then, to the following incredible human beings, guiding lights each one:

Wendy McClure: Thank you being a pioneer in the literary memoir genre (is it now a genre?) with your stellar book *The Wilder Life*. Reading it gave me the spark: *What could I do with MY favorite heroine?* Thanks forever for plowing new ground.

Tim Smith, bookseller extraordinaire and adoptive father, for having coffee with me that February day and showing obvious enthusiasm for this book idea over the others.

Andrea Visser-Bult, PEI native and adoptee, for your unbelievable sermon on God's adoption of us. I sprinkled your wisdom all over this book.

Carissa Woodwyk, for your wisdom, which I found online in a video called *Listen,* is also scattered like good seed throughout these pages.

Pastor David Beelen, for always showing his sheep at Madison Square Church the fatherly love God has for us and for caring deeply about adoption.

To my new friends at Tyndale, I'm so thankful we found one another. Publishing a book with you for the first time has been a joy and a concern—you guys make me bring my best game! Hearty thanks to Jan Long Harris, Beth Vargas, Sharon Leavitt, Cassidy Gage, Nancy Clausen, Todd Starowitz, and the whole clamjamfry (as Maud would say). Marketing and publicity team: I haven't worked much with you yet, but I just know you guys are going to be brilliant!

A special note of gratitude to Stephen Vosloo and his crackerjack team of artists and designers. Your work on this cover elevates the whole book. I adore it!

Jillian VandeWege, you are adorable, fun, and so talented. I have my eyes peeled. You know what I mean. (Clue: *Gobble, gobble . . .*)

Kim Miller, thank you and sweet-banana-pepper blessings on your head for being a genius and knowing when to nip or tuck, add or subtract. Your help in shaping this book was absolutely essential—and so appreciated.

Sarah Atkinson, you are the editor I prayed for, the one who got it immediately. Thank you for going to bat for three card-carrying castaways and for your stalwart support through this book expedition. My prose and storytelling are enriched because of working with you and Kim. You are the wind beneath my wings. But seriously, you kinda are. Are you feeling all the feels?

To my literary agent, Esther Fedorkevich, Ukrainian girls rule the world. We all know that. And you rule the book world, my fireball friend. Thank you for believing in me, my writing, and this idea and for coming through like a top-drawer slap shot in overtime of game seven. (And thanks to Layce for her help with the proposal!)

To Twila Bennett, for being so supportive and encouraging, even though you work for another publisher. Thanks for being willing to help and cheer, always.

To bosom friends like Sheri Rodriguez, who always cheered me on every step of the way, and to Kim Sorelle, for getting us crazy-cheap tickets to the island and for our unforgettable days together in the yellow Fiat on PEI.

Speaking of PEI, I must thank Isabel MacDougall and Claudette MacDonald from Tourism PEI for their gracious and much-appreciated assistance over the course of two trips to the Gentle Island. Also, my gratitude to Shelly Nowak of Canada Post and Cassandra McKinnon of Parks Canada for your help.

To PEI friends Chanel Campbell and Alice VanderZwaag, for welcoming this woman from away to the most beautiful place on earth!

Pamela Campbell, thank you for opening up Silver Bush for us, for allowing us free reign, and for your keen insights into Lucy Maud Montgomery.

Jennie Macneill, thank you for welcoming us into your warm and cozy home on a blustery PEI night. I am more grateful than you know for you opening your heart and telling me about the real Maud, her life, and her funeral. Your insights and wisdom are everywhere in this book.

To The Guild: Alison Hodgson, Angela Blyker, Ann Byle, Cynthia Beach, Sharron Carrns, Shelly Beach, and Tracy Groot, there is no possible way I could have written this book without each one of you. We all know what it's like to traverse this writing life, with its plummy peaks and ghastly desert valleys. You guys were with me in the desert, and for that you have my eternal love and thanks. You are essential to me, and I thank God for His good and perfect gift of our nutty, loving tribe of scribblers.

To David Beach, "Man Guilder." You give birth fathers a good name and show what can happen when a father opens his heart. Thank you for your acute insights into my own birth father and, really, what lies beneath the surface of why fathers renounce their children.

Thank you to my birth mother for stepping up for me many years ago in a very difficult situation. Your bravery gave me life, and for that I will always be grateful.

To my darling mum, Linda Reimer. I love you with all my heart, and I'm so thankful God chose you to be my forever mum. Thank you for your unconditional love and for swiping me from the hospital, even though you didn't have permission!

To Doyle, Jonah, Ezra, and Phoebe: You are my heart. Everything I do, I do it for you. I know, it's a Bryan Adams lyric. But so, so true.

Soli Deo Gloria. Glory to God alone.

Discussion Guide

1. Of all the "Anne" stories, which scene from the books or movies is your favorite? (Or, if you are new to Anne, which anecdote shared in this book makes you most want to read the series and/or watch the movies?)

2. Growing up, Lorilee loved Anne's humor, vigor, and unsinkable spirit. Who were some of your own childhood heroes or heroines from books and movies? What "clicked" for you about those characters? In what ways were they similar to or different from you?

3. Think of some examples of orphanhood in stories for children and young adults. Why do you think it is such a prevalent theme for these age groups? What feelings does it tap into; what situations does it set up; what questions does it provoke?

4. Lorilee associates the words *bereft, left behind*, and *left* with *orphan*. Do you agree with her that, by that association, we've all been orphans at one time or another? If yes, how has that been true in your own life?

5. How do Lorilee's trips to two special places—Prince Edward Island and Korea—inspire her and alter the course of her life? What has been the most meaningful trip or adventure you've ever taken, and what made it so significant to you?

6. Lorilee traces Anne's connections to her first "bosom friend," Diana Barry, as well as the snarky Josie Pye, and shares parallel relationships from her own life. Who was your first "bosom friend"? What drew the two of you together? And were you ever targeted by a Josie Pye? What did each relationship teach you about the meaning of friendship, the sense of belonging, and how to treat others? If you are a parent, how do those relationships inform your reaction when your own kids form new friendships or get picked on?

7. When she was lonely as a child, Lorilee fantasized about being rescued by her birth mother, saying, "There has always been a pattern with me: Whenever my confidence and heart are at a low ebb, I wish and wonder the most about lost connections and what might have been." Can you relate? What "lost connections" in your own life come to mind?

8. What difficulties do Lorilee and Doyle encounter in their marriage, and what happens to lead Lorilee to her "book of Revelation"? How does it connect to Anne's? What do their reactions and decisions reveal about their personal characters, how they have grown, and what becomes most important to them?

9. When actor Jonathan Crombie died in April 2015, the outpouring of love and grief proved how much the character of Gilbert Blythe (and Crombie's portrayal) meant to people.

Why do you think there was such an enormous response? How did you respond when you heard that Crombie had died?

10. Why does Lorilee struggle with the question, "Are you Phoebe's real mom?" What does she mean when she says she loves her adopted daughter "biologically"? What do you personally think it means to be a "real" mom, and why?

11. When Lorilee reaches out to her biological parents, what does she fear or hope will result? What does she learn about herself through her contact with Dora, and later, Tom? How is her faith in God affected by what happens? How do you think you might have responded if you were in her shoes?

12. The title of this book links Lorilee and her daughter with one of their favorite stories. If you and your own mom or daughter were going to write about an adventure together (based on a literary classic or otherwise), what do you think it might be called? Why?

13. Describe Lorilee's relationship with her adoptive parents and brother. How would you compare it to the role that Matthew and Marilla Cuthbert play in Anne's story? How do Matthew and Marilla balance each other to give Anne what she needs at different times and in different ways, and what can this teach us about our own role in the lives of the people we love?

14. Describing Phoebe's "Korean mama" to her daughter, Lorilee says she "did the right thing by taking wonderful care of you when you were in her tummy. . . . She loved you very much and was so brave." What difficulties did Moon face as a young, unwed mother-to-be? What choices did she make, and what

support (or lack thereof) did she experience? Why do you think Lorilee senses she is "bestowing a great gift to [Phoebe's] heart" through sharing this story of her birth mother?

15. What common threads do you see in Lorilee's, Anne's, and Phoebe's journeys? What links do they share with your own life? What do the three orphans' stories ultimately reveal about what it means to find your family?

16. Why do you think Lorilee chose two Bible verses, John 14:18 and Isaiah 49:15-16, as the opening epigraphs for this book? How do they tie in to the overarching theme of the book? As you read them, what do they say to you personally?

17. What would you say is the central question this memoir asks—and how would you answer it?

Notes

INTRODUCTION

1. Quotations throughout are from *Anne of Green Gables* or *Anne of the Island*, published as Bantam reissues in 1992; originally published in 1908 and 1915 by Lucy Maud Montgomery. L. M. Montgomery, *Anne of Green Gables* (New York, NY: Bantam Books, 1992), 178.
2. A reference to one of the classic scenes in *The Princess Bride*. After Vizzini once again cries, "Inconceivable!" Inigo tells him, "You keep using that word. I do not think it means what you think it means." Likewise, I think *orphan* is a word we often toss around without considering its deeper meanings.
3. *Bartlett's Roget's Thesaurus*, s.v. 750.7 "remaining."
4. For more information on L. M. Montgomery, check out the L. M. Montgomery Institute online at www.lmmontgomery.ca.
5. Montgomery, *Anne of Green Gables*, 176.
6. Ibid., 26.
7. Ibid., 37.
8. Ibid., 12.

CHAPTER 1

1. Montgomery, *Anne of Green Gables*, 2.
2. Ibid., 4.
3. Ibid., 3.
4. Ibid., 5.
5. Ibid.
6. Ibid., 7.
7. Ibid.
8. Ibid.
9. Ibid.
10. Ibid., 10.

CHAPTER 2

1. L. M. Montgomery, *Anne of the Island* (New York, NY: Bantam Books, 1992), 147.
2. Ibid., 148.
3. Ibid.

4. Some scholars believe Bertha and Walter died of typhoid; though others think Anne's reference to "fever" refers to scarlet fever.
5. L. M. Montgomery, *The Annotated Anne of Green Gables,* ed. Wendy E. Barry, Margaret Anne Doody, and Mary E. Doody Jones (New York: Oxford University Press, 1997), 423.
6. Ibid., 424–425.

CHAPTER 3
1. Carissa Woodwyk, "Listen," accessed April 29, 2015, https://vimeo.com/73044194.
2. "Brain Scan Shows Rejection Pain," *BBC News,* October 10, 2003. Accessed April 8, 2015, http://news.bbc.co.uk/2/hi/health/3178242.stm.
3. Montgomery, *Anne of Green Gables,* 86.
4. Ibid., 107.
5. Oxford Dictionaries, accessed April 29, 2015, http://www.oxforddictionaries.com/definition/english/ebullition.
6. Montgomery, *Anne of Green Gables,* 110.
7. Ibid., 305.
8. Ibid., 187.
9. Ibid., 258.
10. Ibid., 289.
11. Ibid., 244.
12. Ibid., 218.
13. Ibid., 219.

CHAPTER 4
1. Montgomery, *Anne of Green Gables,* 87.
2. Ibid., 87.
3. Ibid., 88.
4. Ibid., 109.
5. Ibid., 114.
6. Ibid., 119.
7. Ibid., 153.
8. Irene Gammel, *Looking for Anne of Green Gables* (New York: St. Martin's, 2008), 118.
9. Ibid., 150.
10. Ibid., 176.
11. In fact, *The Alpine Path* is the title of the book that L. M. Montgomery wrote about her own writing career.
12. Montgomery, *Anne of Green Gables,* 210.
13. Ibid., 210.

CHAPTER 5
1. See http://shopatsullivan.com/gilbert-throw-pillow.html, accessed March 13, 2015.
2. See comments section in Lorilee Craker, "A Eulogy for Gilbert Blythe," *Peace, Love & Raspberry Cordial,* April 18, 2015, http://lorileecraker.com/2015/04/a-eulogy-for-gilbert-blythe/.

3. "Mr. Blythe," *Anne and Gilbert: The Musical*, Water Street Records, 2006.
4. Montgomery, *Anne of Green Gables*, 111.
5. Ibid., 111.
6. Ibid., 112.
7. Ibid., 113.
8. Ibid., 115.
9. Ibid., 136.
10. Ibid., 154.
11. Anne refers to Gilbert this way in chapters 19 and 25.
12. Montgomery, *Anne of Green Gables*, 225.
13. Ibid., 307.
14. Montgomery, *Anne of the Island*, 237.
15. Ibid., 237.
16. Perceval is the hero of a short story Anne wrote and discusses with Diana in chapter 12, "Averil's Atonement," in *Anne of the Island*.
17. Montgomery, *Anne of the Island*, 236.

CHAPTER 6
1. Montgomery, *Anne of the Island*, 46.
2. Montgomery, *Anne of Green Gables*, 12.
3. Ibid., 156.
4. Ibid., 273.
5. L. M. Montgomery, *The Selected Journals of L. M. Montgomery, Vol. 1: 1889–1910*, ed. Mary Rubio and Elizabeth Waterston (Don Mills, Ontario: Oxford Press, 1985), 235.
6. In *The Alpine Path*, Maud explained that Rachel was based on the experiences of her father's cousin, Eliza Montgomery.
7. L. M. Montgomery, *The Selected Journals of L. M. Montgomery*, Vol II: 1910–1921., ed. Mary Rubio and Elizabeth Waterston (Don Mills, Ontario: Oxford University Press, 1987), 250.
8. Out of respect for their privacy, the names of members of my birth family have been replaced with pseudonyms. Some identifying details have been changed as well.
9. Frederick Buechner, *Beyond Words: Daily Readings in the ABCs of Faith* (New York: HarperOne, 2004), 383.

CHAPTER 9
1. Montgomery, *Anne of Green Gables*, 64.
2. Mrs. Rachel's precise critique was this: "She's terrible skinny and homely, Marilla. Come here, child, and let me have a look at you. Lawful heart, did any one ever see such freckles? And hair as red as carrots!" Montgomery, *Anne of Green Gables*, 64.
3. Ibid., 65.
4. Ibid.
5. Ibid., 16.
6. Ibid., 60.
7. Ibid., 267.

8. Ibid., 65.
9. Ibid., 66.
10. Ibid., 68.
11. Ibid., 146.
12. Ibid., 73.

CHAPTER 10
1. See Galatians 5:22-23.

CHAPTER 11
1. *Freiwilliges* translates as "volunteer" in German, and at a wedding or funeral, you never know who might "volunteer" their poetry, songs, skits, and memories. Doyle calls them "Fried Villagers," and I believe this free-for-all of talent (and lack of it) is singular to the Mennonites.
2. L. M. Montgomery, *Emily of New Moon*, chapter 3, "A Hop Out of Kin."
3. Ibid.
4. Ibid.

CHAPTER 12
1. Montgomery, *Anne of Green Gables*, 125.
2. Ibid., 123.
3. Ibid., 121.
4. Ibid., 127.
5. Ibid., 130.
6. Ibid., 130.
7. Ibid., 138.
8. Ibid., 172.
9. Ibid., 176.
10. John Stonestreet, "A Stunning Pro-Life Documentary," commentary, *Breakpoint*, February 27, 2015, http://www.breakpoint.org/bpcommentaries/entry/13/26942.

CHAPTER 13
1. Montgomery, *Anne of the Island*, 145.
2. Ibid., 146.
3. Ibid.
4. Ibid., 147.
5. Ibid.
6. Ibid.
7. Ibid.
8. Ibid., 148.

CHAPTER 15
1. See Isaiah 49:16.

CHAPTER 16
1. Montgomery, *Anne of Green Gables*, 196.
2. Ibid., 196.

3. Ibid., 197.
4. Ibid., 197.
5. Ibid., 199.
6. Ibid., 199.
7. Ibid., 200.
8. Ibid.
9. Ibid., 203.
10. Ibid., 292.
11. Ibid., 292.
12. Ibid., 274.
13. See 1 Corinthians 13.

CHAPTER 17
1. This poetic-sounding phrase is not merely an accurate description of the island; historians believe it was the first name given to it by the native Mi'kmaq. They called their home Abegweit, or "land cradled by waves." See http://www.virtualcountries.com/blog/book-a-holiday-on-prince -edward-island.
2. This quotation comes from one of the display cases at the post office.
3. These two quotes come from L. M. Montgomery, *The Alpine Path*.
4. Marilla "looked like a woman of narrow experience and rigid conscience, which she was; but there was a saving something about her mouth which, if it had been ever so slightly developed, might have been considered indicative of a sense of humor." Montgomery, *Anne of Green Gables*, 5.
5. Ibid., 303.
6. Mary Henley Rubio, *Lucy Maud Montgomery: The Gift of Wings* (Toronto: Doubleday Canada, 2010), 576.
7. For more on the discussion of how L. M. Montgomery died, see Irene Gammel, "The Fatal Disappointments of Lucy Maud," *Globe and Mail*, November 15, 2008. See also "L. M. Montgomery Suicide Revealed," *CBC News*, September 22, 2008, http://www.cbc.ca/news/canada/prince-edward-island/l-m-montgomery -suicide-revealed-1.723426.
8. L. M. Montgomery, "Each in His Own Tongue," in *Chronicles of Avonlea* (New York: Bantam, 1993), 57.
9. Ibid., 63–64.
10. Ibid., 64.
11. Ibid., 65.
12. Ibid., 67.
13. Ibid., 68.
14. Rubio, *Lucy Maud Montgomery*, 576.

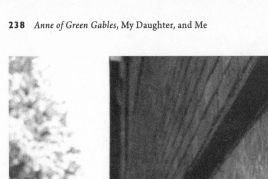

Lorilee and Phoebe Craker, June 2015

About the Author

Lorilee Craker is the author of more than a dozen books, including *A Is for Atticus: Baby Names from Great Books*, *Money Secrets of the Amish* (an Audie Awards finalist, which she wrote and narrated), and the *New York Times* bestseller *Through the Storm* with Lynne Spears. A freelance journalist, blogger, and speaker, Lorilee was an entertainment writer for the *Grand Rapids Press* for seventeen years. She has been featured in many media outlets, including the *Wall Street Journal*, *Time*, and *People*. The proud founder of a writing day camp for middle schoolers, Lorilee lives in Grand Rapids, Michigan, with her husband, Doyle, and their three children: Jonah, Ezra, and Phoebe.